Many Blessings

"*Leaving the Land of Me* is powerfully inspirational and right on time. Kudos to Katheryn Saunders for reminding us how, when grounded in faith, simple acts of kindness can change lives."

- Donald Gerard, Author of *Collective Wisdom: Powerful Stories and Practical Advice for Achieving Success*

Leaving the Land of Me

The Little Things Do Matter

Katheryn Saunders

Dewey Decimal Classification: 248
Subject Heading: CHRISTIAN EXPERIENCE / PRACTICE / LIFE

Unless otherwise noted, all Scripture quotations are taken from the
Holy Bible, New International Version, copyright © 1973, 1978, 1984
by International Bible Society.
Published by Zondervan Corporation

Dedication

I dedicate this book my husband Craig. From the very beginning, even when I didn't think I was capable, he encouraged me to keep pressing on. God smiled on me the day I met him. I'm blessed to be his wife.

I also want to thank all of our Pastors for shepherding me, and Ray for inspiring the title.

Table of Contents

Message from the Author

About four years ago, I felt God pressing me to begin recording the stories of some amazing people I have met throughout my life. I have learned so many things from each of them, and I was beginning to forget both the stories and the lessons. At first I resisted–the thought of documenting all those stories seemed a bit overwhelming. God tends to win arguments however, and eventually I gave in. The process of writing this book lasted a couple of years, writing early in the morning when my children were still asleep, or when I had a spare hour or two, but the manuscript is finally complete. This book is short and easy to read, but it is packed with life lessons and encouragement for anyone ready to consider stepping outside of himself and the world to which he's accustomed. The experience can be life-changing.

You will find that I use both the terms "serve" and "volunteer" in this book, because different people view this work from different perspectives. Some people use the terms interchangeably, but for me the difference is one's motivation. Technically, the term "volunteer" isn't Biblical, but it's an easy way to describe community service. You will find that I use the term "serve" more often than not, however, because those actions come from a place of wanting to serve God by caring for those He loves, (which is everyone by the way). In addition, please note that this book was written for the purpose of encouraging you to begin stepping outside your own circumstances and to start noticing and interacting with those around you. Because of questions that arise when you serve, I believe it's good to be firm in your faith before you begin. If you aren't, my prayer is that you will encounter God in the process, and seek to know Him better.

Throughout the book, I share stories that came to me either directly or indirectly. I don't use last names (except in cases where the contributors lead non-profits). Also, in some cases, I changed first names (for stories of a more sensitive nature), or if individuals made that request while granting me permission to include their story. I have also included my impressions of some exceptional non-profits. Some are Christian organizations and some are not. These are my impressions only. I include their contact information in the back of the book in order for you to visit their websites and gather more detailed information for yourself. I hope you enjoy my book, *Leaving the Land of Me: The Little Things Do Matter.*

9

Preface

Indulge me for a moment. Visualize the little person who exists somewhere in all of our psyches. His voice is the one that tells us we are only one person, that we can't possibly make a difference in the world. His voice also tells us that we don't have the time, skills, experience, or money to change another person's life. Let's call that little guy George. Well, I hate to be the one to tell you this, but you need to know. Are you ready? Maybe you better sit down. George is a liar.

This book was written to dispel the myth that one person can't change the world. It simply isn't true. A ripple effect happens when we are kind to another human being. That kindness changes us, and it changes them. I've seen it more times than I can count. Sometimes, it's the smallest thing, and other times monumental, but the change happens.

Over the years I have had the great privilege of meeting many amazing people. Some of them were volunteers and some of them were people whose lives were changed by someone they didn't know. All of them had something to teach me. This book tells stories of those teachers, people like Darren who was buried up to his neck and left to die during the killing fields in Cambodia, and Thaddeus who chooses to live on the streets in order to help homeless people beat their drug addictions. Also included in this book are stories of people who offered a simple smile or touch that changed a life, and they didn't have to be millionaires or saints to have an impact. I've made more mistakes than I care to count, but therein lies the beauty of life. Our imperfections provide us with a source of empathy. Our humanness creates connections. We're all in this together.

Leaving the Land of Me is about stepping outside one's self for a moment. It's about taking the focus off our own personal challenges and struggles for a time and directing our focus and energy toward another human soul. That ebb and flow–love in, love out–is like the breath of God moving around in the world. It fuels that which connects us, one to another. All it takes is a prayerful shift in thinking.

The bottom line? We need to find our way back to humanity. One person can change the world. It starts with you.

Chapter 1

―――― ※ ――――

Daisy Picking

Jessie was a daisy picker. You know the one, blonde pigtails, standing in the middle of the soccer field staring at the little white daisies smiling at her from the grass below. Meanwhile, the other girls raced by, soccer ball flying, focused intensely on the goal. Occasionally, she would stop picking daisies to chat with one of the girls on the other team. "I like your ponytail holder," she'd say. "Would you like to be my friend?"

I was always content with this arrangement. She seemed to be having a good time, a little fresh air for my daughter while I enjoyed a nice latte and some conversation with the other moms. My husband, on the other hand, has the heart of a champion, a true competitor. Every fiber of his being strives to win. That dear man sat patiently through more daisy picking than I care to remember. "You're getting better!" he'd muster up. Then he always found at least one positive thing she did during the game to try and motivate her. And let me tell you, since she was completely disengaged from the game most of the time, finding anything to encourage her was a stretch to say the least. "I like the way you swing your arms when you run," he'd say.

Now you have to understand that it probably drove my husband to the brink of insanity to sit quietly week after week while my darling girl happily selected the daisies with the most petals. One day, after about twenty minutes of daisy picking, I looked over, and noticed that he had a strange expression on his face–a kind of strained, frustrated, face turning purple sort of look. Actually, he looked like he was going to spontaneously implode. All of a sudden, he stood up, cupped his hands over his mouth, and yelled at the top of his lungs, "Jessie, if you score a goal, I will buy you a car!"

I am just going tell you right now that I laughed so hard I thought I'd pee in my pants. And I wasn't the only one. The whole crowd was in hysterics, not at Jess, but at my husband. And I do mean everyone-our team's parents, the other team's parents, all the players on both teams.

First of all, you need to know that my daughter was six years old at the time. What possessed my husband to offer her a car was beyond me.

13

But I must tell you that Jessie is and always has been a planner. This child thinks ahead. I looked at her, and she had this funny little grin on her face. A look of knowing, as if to say "Oh, well that's all you want? Something so irrelevant? Just a goal?" I could almost see the little wheels turning inside her head. "Hmm… I *will* need a car one day…" Then something amazing happened. With very clear purpose and intention, I saw her turn to see who had the ball. She began to run full speed in that direction. Before I could even grasp what was happening, my daughter, the daisy picker, stole the ball from the girl who had it, ran down the field with it *at full speed*, weaving in and out of every child standing in her way, and slammed it into the goal with such force the goalie couldn't have stopped it if she wanted to.

You have never seen such an eruption in your entire life. The crowd went wild. The parents on both sides jumped to their feet cheering and yelling for Jessie. All the girls from both teams offered high fives, asking "What kind of car are you going to buy?" I turned to look at my husband. There he sat, mouth agape, dumbfounded. Maybe he was thinking about how much that goal was going to cost him. Or maybe he was trying to wrap his brain around the fact that in two years of soccer, his daughter could have been running, blocking, and scoring goals, but for some bizarre reason beyond his comprehension, she had chosen not to. I may never know.

For me, however, it was one of those moments as a parent when you learn a profound and life-changing lesson from your child. I know that girls tend to be relational. Some of us are more competitive than others. I think, though, as a gender, we are slightly more focused on the people in our lives— family, friends, and business and community relationships. Everything else, including the tasks themselves, although important, is peripheral. But I never imagined that a child could act with such intention. She had been standing in the middle of a battlefield and had chosen not to participate, knowing full well that a crowd of people probably thought she was incapable of doing what was expected, and choosing to do, instead, what felt right and good to her. She opted for making a new friend and complementing someone (from the other team, heaven forbid) on her ponytail holder. Instead, she chose to delight in a beautiful little white daisy. It was an "aha" moment for me, to say the least.

Now I do understand that soccer is a sport, and if you are going to sign up, you should probably actually play the game, but go with me for a moment. I'm speaking metaphorically here. How often do we get so caught in the business of daily life, that we begin paying more attention to what the world expects of us and less attention to our inner voice? When all is said and done, and our lives draw to a close, what will matter most to us? Will we care more about whether we accomplished our goals and did what the world asked of us, or about our relationships and the people whose paths we crossed along the way? As a Christian, I sometimes worry that we have forgotten Christ's message about the importance of being in relationship with one another. The world views us as separated not only from people of other faiths, but also from each other. Gandhi said, "I like your Christ. I don't like your Christians. Your Christians are so unlike your Christ." This saddens me because Christ clearly modeled that our relationships (even with those we don't necessarily agree with) should mimic the oneness that exists in the Trinity. We need to remember that God (the Spirit) is in us. It's a matter of knowing it and living it. Remembering this, we should treat all those who cross our paths with kindness, love and respect.

I come from a long line of people who understand the importance of serving and human connection. It's such an integral part of my history. My grandparents were involved with The Oral Hull Foundation for the Blind. As a child, I remember riding around in the car with my grandmother, visiting blind women to see if they needed anything. They made me the most beautiful scarves and hats to wear. I was fascinated by the idea that someone without sight could create something so perfect. When I was little, my grandparents helped raise enough money to build a large facility where the blind could swim, walk in the garden and enjoy descriptions in Braille of the flowers as they touched them. They could also ride bikes outside attached to a special apparatus. I spent hours at this facility with my grandparents having a wonderful time. My father was a member of the Lion's Club, and my mother was involved with an organization called PEO. My brother and I volunteered each summer at the County Fair Lions Booth flipping burgers and making milk shakes. (I use the term "volunteer" loosely, as it was actually under threat of yard work and other forms of manual labor from my father.) Those kinds of activities, whether self-imposed or forced by Dad, permeated the landscape of our family terrain. And as I grew, I began to find joy in the work.

I started my own personal journey of service just out of college. My first experience was as a Big Sister to an incredible little girl named Clarese. The first day I met her, she ran to get her violin and she played for me. I'd never met a kid so clever. That child (at age eight) could give me driving directions to almost anywhere in town! We baked cookies, and we went to movies. I even taught her how to hold her breath while diving into a pool. (We practiced holding our breath in the bathroom sink). We were together for quite a few years, but eventually I married and had my own children, and it became more difficult to spend time regularly with Clarese. Nevertheless, has been my privilege to know her. I attended her wedding recently, what a beautiful bride! She grew up to be a phenomenal woman.

I later enjoyed working for a program called Little Bit Special Riders. (Little Bit Special Riders is a program that helps disabled children ride horses.) Mostly, I worked with a blind girl who was quite accomplished as a rider. Hopping on that horse gave her a freedom she couldn't enjoy on foot. Some of the children were paraplegic, some had cerebral palsy, and others were blind or deaf. I remember closing my eyes and trying to imagine what it must feel like for them to run for the first time and feel the wind whip across their cheeks and through their hair. An exhilarated smile would spread across the children's faces that seemed to light the whole arena. I'd see that smile and feel my heart explode. And, to be honest, I also loved working with the horses. They can be such gentle giants. I always felt they knew the children were special, and they seemed so careful not to harm them in any way.

And then there was Habitat for Humanity. I heard they were looking for a volunteer fundraiser, so I showed up one night for a meeting. In what seemed like the blink of an eye, I found that I had been there fourteen years. My tenure with Habitat for Humanity turned out to be so much more than I expected. My greatest privilege was meeting the families. I would sit with them, enthralled as they shared their life stories with me. Habitat really does change people's lives. Several years ago, my husband Craig (who is a firefighter and does some work with real estate on the side) had been praying for a way to serve. He wanted to get more involved in the community and in our church, but he wasn't sure what to do. One day, while he was at work, his station got a call for an elderly man who had been up on a ladder trying to get the leaves out of his gutters. The man had fallen off the ladder and broken his back. Finding this elderly man who had injured himself while laboring on his home was the inspiration Craig had been looking for. We both love senior citizens, and, with Craig's background in construction and my experience with Habitat, the direction was obvious. Consequently, in September of 2004, we started an outreach program that does free home maintenance and repairs for senior citizens. We decided that we would recruit some other firefighter families to volunteer and let the church refer seniors to us. Soon after we began our outreach program, we met with the church and learned that the pastoral staff had been praying for someone to do this work. Calls had been pouring in for help, but the church had no one to whom to send the calls. It's amazing how God works. Within six months, we had over fifty volunteers signed up to work with us, and off we went! Like most volunteer organizations, we've waxed and waned, plugging along, learning as we go. My administrative skills leave a lot to be desired. When I think of all the gutters cleaned, handicapped ramps built, and leaky toilets and roofs repaired, however, it all seems worthwhile. I share these things with you not to toot my own horn in any way, but to tell you that these experiences have been a great source of joy in my life. The work itself is extremely fulfilling, but I've found so much more than that. I discovered what it means to be "God in skin" to someone in need. And those connections–the "moments" I shared with another human being–were more precious to me than any other part of the work itself.

My husband and I attend a church near our home. One of the reasons we chose this particular church was its involvement in the community. "Loving God Loving Others" is printed on everything you see. And their actions match their words. We feel at home there. As a church body, we spend a lot of time out in the community serving wherever we are needed. Through the church, we've connected with small groups as well.

Once a week, I get together for a Bible study with a group of women. Sometimes we get a lot accomplished, and sometimes we don't. Always, however, the conversations are thought provoking. A while back, the church offered a special series on serving, and our group followed along with a book and DVD each week. Somewhere along the line, we got on the subject of "the little things." Yes, we all do community service as much as we can, but are we too busy to notice the little things? Are we so caught up in the day-to-day activities that make up our lives that we forget to open our eyes and notice the people around us? Perhaps, it's like having tunnel vision. There's always that check-list.

Now I have to fess up. For me, there is something extremely gratifying about producing a to-do list each morning, happily checking off items as the day goes on. This process gives me a feeling of accomplishment. I have even created a point system, and I assign higher point values to items that are particularly disgusting or time consuming. For example, washing my teenage son's soccer socks– which probably have a toxicity level equal only to Chernobyl–has to be worth at least fifty points. For every so many points, I reward myself with a cupcake from my favorite cupcake shop. (Yes, I do realize that is just wrong in so many ways.) At the end of the day, however, although gratified at the completion of the day's list–and even more gratified with my cupcake–I began to feel dissatisfied with what I really accomplished that day. Yes, I picked up the jumbo-sized container of ketchup for my son, the scrambled eggs and ketchup addict, but did I notice the elderly woman whose car had broken down along side the road? Yes, I had a productive day at work. Yes, I gave myself a hundred points that night for cleaning out the refrigerator, but as I looked out the kitchen window at the neighbor's house with leaf-filled gutters, did I think about him? Why doesn't anyone ever visit him? My friends felt the same way.

"What if," we asked one day, "we were willing to stop what we were doing for five minutes and respond to those with whom we come in contact? What if we began taking our eyes off the 'list' and started making eye contact with people in line at Starbucks. What would happen?" What transpired over the next few weeks changed not only my perception of time but its value as well.

During the first week, my friend Dawn had a pretty amazing experience. Monday morning she was out the door, list in one hand, daughter Hannah in the other, headed for the grocery store. Hannah needed to be at school in thirty minutes, so she had just enough time to dash in and grab what she needed. Dawn flew through the produce section, barely noticing the old man standing alone in the apple section, staring at the Fujis. "He's probably trying to make up his mind," she told herself. "We do live in Washington, the apple capital of the universe," she thought as she scooted off to the bakery department. But as she reached for the last item on her list, she felt compelled to peek around the corner and see if he was still there. There he stood, unmoved. Partly because of what we'd been talking about, and partly (in my opinion) a nudge from God, Dawn walked over and gently placed her hand on the man's shoulder.

"Excuse me sir, can I help you choose an apple?" She asked. There was no response. It was then that Dawn leaned in to make eye contact with the man, and as she did, she saw tears rolling down his face. "What's wrong?" she asked. "Why are you crying?" It took a while for him to answer, and then quietly the man said, "I miss my wife. I wanted to bake a pie," he said, as the tears continued to flow. Apparently, he thought he'd

18

reached the point where he could do this–go out into the world without his best friend–but it was just too much. He found himself stuck there, unable to move. Dawn put her arm around the man and listened (now with Dawn crying also) as he told her how his beautiful wife of many years had died recently. He told Dawn how his heart ached for her beyond comprehension.

And there, in the produce section of the grocery store, something incredible happened–a human connection. Dawn could have just gone on about her day. The old man could have remained there unnoticed, unloved. Instead, she was love to him that day. Love incarnate. Isn't that why we are here? We seem, as a society, to be on this path of isolation from one another. People in my grandmother's generation–even in my parents' generation when they were younger–were so aware of each other. They were connected. People said "hello" when they passed on the street. They asked each other, "How are you?" and genuinely wanted to know the answer. Those relationships and human contact were much more important than getting through a to-do list.

Dawn and Mr. Jacobs talked for a while that day. Tears dried. She asked if he had family around and he did. "Just a bad day," he said and thanked her for seeing him through that moment. She helped him select the apples for his pie and gave him a hug. But mostly, she noticed an old man standing in the apple section of the grocery store crying–and she did something about it.

Five Little Things

1. Buy someone a cupcake.
There seem to be little cupcake shops cropping up everywhere. They do such a beautiful job of putting cupcakes in lovely boxes wrapped up with ribbons. Give a cupcake to your favorite grocery store clerk or barista. Thank them for always doing such a good job. Or set a cupcake on someone's desk at work with a nice note. You'll brighten their day.

2. Rake a neighbor's leaves.
Find a neighbor who's a busy single mom, an elderly person, or just someone who could use the help, and rake up their leaves or mow their lawn. Tell them you just wanted to lighten their load a little. You might make a new friend.

3. Read to a senior citizen.
Stop by your local retirement home and ask if there is anyone to whom you might read. Set up a time to go periodically and read to that person. You could even form a book club where you do the reading.

4. Buy someone a latte.
I was standing in line recently at my favorite coffee place when I noticed an elderly man sitting at a table looking out the window. This particular place was in a grocery store, and I imagined that he'd finished his shopping and was waiting for his ride. He looked tired, he wasn't smiling, and he didn't have a cup of coffee. The man in front of me walked over to him and asked if he could buy him a cup of coffee while he waited for his ride. The man looked shocked at first, but then smiled and happily accepted. Buy someone a cup of coffee today.

5. Buy a soldier lunch.
Next time you are having a meal at a restaurant or fast food place and you see a soldier there, anonymously purchase his/her meal and tell the waiter to thank the soldier for selflessly serving their country. Regardless of how you feel about war, service men and women, and their families, make huge sacrifices daily on our behalf.

Chapter 2

_❋_

Hiding in Plain Sight

I love children—all shapes and sizes. Children are terrific. If someone has one leg, they ask the person how their leg came off, and by the way, would they like to play. They spontaneously break out in song in the middle of the grocery store. They pick their nose in front of God and everybody. Children are so open, so unaware of the rules we've given ourselves as adults. Who came up with these rules, anyway? Here are a few of my personal favorites:

1. Never talk to someone who looks weird. You will definitely be accosted.
2. When walking down the street, don't make eye contact. You are busy and someone might start a conversation with you.
3. That guy standing by the side of the road holding a sign? Drug addict.
4. Most importantly, old people are cute, but never start a conversation with one. You will be there for a minimum of three hours.

Does any of this sound familiar? Oh, come on. It's kind of funny to say out loud, but most of us (if we are going to be honest) have thought these things at one point or another. Of course they are ridiculous generalizations, but it's what we tell ourselves to get through that silly list each day. We make assumptions for a variety of reasons, some of which are valid. Every once in a while, however, I get knocked over the head by my own skewed assumptions, and frankly, by my own ambivalence. Take the greeter at church, for example.

Greeters are the wonderful people who stand at the doors to the church and offer a handshake and a cheerful "Good morning!" They make the congregation feel welcome and wanted. Rain or shine, every weekend, there they are with a ready smile. I never thought much about the greeters before. Remember when you were in kindergarten and you thought your teacher lived at the school? It was sort of like that for me. They probably have little beds in the back, a bar of soap, some breakfast muffins and *voila!* There they are at church on Sunday morning.

One of our greeters is an elderly man who has the kindest face. You can tell by his demeanor that he is a positive, upbeat person. That man is so faithful to his position. I can't remember ever going to church when he wasn't there. I'm ashamed to admit that I don't know his name, but if he happens to be standing by the door I go in, I (like everyone else) always smile back, shake his hand and say "Good morning." One morning, though, something happened. I'm not sure exactly why, but I've never forgotten it. As we piled out of the car that morning, the kids ran off to Sunday school, and Craig and I headed to the front doors. From a distance I could see him standing in the doorway smiling, shaking people's hands. As I neared him, though, I felt a wave of gratitude. "That dear man is so devoted, so unselfish," I thought. "He must have days when he doesn't feel like greeting, but there he is anyway." Suddenly I felt so happy to see him, so grateful for his willingness to serve in this way. I guess I must have been wearing this huge smile on my face, because as I approached him, he opened his arms to me, wrapped me up and gave me a huge hug. I hugged him back. There we stood, the greeter and me, hugging each other. I have no idea why, but that hug seemed to fill my soul. When we stopped hugging, I stepped back. "Thank you for the hug!" I said. "How did I get so lucky?" "You smiled at me." he said. "That's all?" I thought to myself. Everyone smiled at him. We had been attending that church for nine years at the time, and I can't remember seeing him give anyone a hug before. I must have looked puzzled when I said, "I smiled at you?" There was a pause, and then he said, "You meant it." as he turned to smile and greet the next person.

I felt the earth shift. Had I been walking in my sleep? It was as if God was saying "Wake up! Open your eyes!" How much more I had missed? With how many other people in my life was I having sleepwalking experiences? The grocery clerk? The person at the coffee house? The mail man? Oh, we smile and say "hello," and "fine, thank you." Blah, blah, blah. Most of the time, though, we are on autopilot. We probably couldn't even describe how they looked. Most likely we don't know anything personal about them. Why not? Does it really take that long to compliment someone or ask if they have any fun plans for the weekend?

Between Dawn's experience in the grocery store and mine with the greeter I decided I needed a wake-up call. That night I asked God to open my eyes. I felt I was doing a good job of serving as a volunteer, but I wasn't sure I had been *really* seeing those I served. Maybe I was missing what really mattered–those human connections. I asked Him not only to help me do a better job of noticing people and making a connection with them, but also to respond if they were in need. I didn't want praise for it. I just wanted a moment. I asked for an opportunity to give someone a little faith in human kindness. I don't know why what happened next surprised me. "Ask and you shall receive."

The next morning, I headed out for the day, turning down the main street that leads out of our neighborhood. This particular street has a series of hills going up and down with little side streets branching off, where most of the houses are. As I came down one of the hills, I saw a man I didn't know (one of the neighbors) whose car had stalled right in the middle of one of those hills. He was desperately trying to push the car back up the hill and around the corner to his house, while also trying to steer it. "Wake up, Kathy," I thought. I quickly pulled over in front of where his car was, stepped out of my car, put my hands on the front bumper and began to push. Between him and me, within seconds the car was up the hill and parked safely in front of his house. "I can't thank you enough!" said the man. "I was beginning to think no one would stop." We said a quick hello and introduced ourselves. "Hope your day gets better," I said and was on my way. As I drove off, I wondered if the day before I might have driven by, not even noticing him.

The next day, I had to do some work in a nearby town and was driving along a busy four-lane road. There seemed to be some kind of chaos up ahead, because people were honking their car horns. As I approached the area, I saw that an elderly man had lost all the plywood out of the back of his truck, and the wood was lying all over the road. People in his lane were swerving around the plywood and honking their horns as they went by. The people in my lane were getting agitated as well. "There it is," I thought, and pulled to the side of the road. The man was trying hard to pick it up, but if you have ever tried to maneuver large sheets of plywood by yourself, you know that it's really awkward. I grabbed one end of a piece and said, "Let's do it together." He looked very relieved as he grabbed the other end and we began to load. Then something wonderful happened! A young man who was driving by saw us and pulled over his truck. He ran over and started to help. Then a husband and wife pulled over and out they came. There we were, the five of us, complete strangers loading plywood. Within minutes the truck was full. The young man helped him tie the wood in, so it wouldn't happen again. We smiled and wished each other a great day. When I got back into my car, I thanked God for that opportunity.

On day three, I woke up excited to see what would happen next. As I went about my day though, I almost felt disappointed as it drew to a close and nothing had happened. On the way home, I stopped by a Mexican restaurant that my family likes for take-out. As I climbed back into my car, I began rearranging the containers so they wouldn't spill. All of a sudden there was a knock at my car window. I looked up and saw a woman standing there. I rolled down my window and said hello. "Do you have a few dollars I could use for gas?" she said. "I ran out of gas and need to get my kids home." I didn't see any car, and I didn't see any kids. Now this was a big one for me. I struggle with this. What if she was lying? Am I supporting a drug or alcohol habit? What is the right thing to do? My friend Sel likes to remind me (when I'm trying to decide whether or not to help someone in need) that Mathew 25:40 says, "I tell you the truth, whatever you did for one of the least of these brothers of mine, you did for me." In other words, when I do something for someone in need, I'm doing it for God. I thought about this for a moment and decided to respond. I almost never have any cash, so I told myself that I would look, and if I was supposed to give her money, it would be there. I opened my wallet and there was $5.00. I handed it to her. "Thank you so much. God bless you." She said. And He had.

I have no way of knowing how she spent the money that day, and frankly, how the money was spent is irrelevant. I realized that night that there are times when a simple act of kindness is enough to offer a glimmer of hope to someone feeling hopeless. As we respond to people in our environment, the invisible line that separates "us" from "them" begins to evaporate. We don't always need to know the outcome. I think sometimes we do things for the response rather than the doing itself. When we reach a point where the act itself is enough, our perspective begins to change.

We've all heard the expression before. "There, but by the grace of God, go I." One of our pastors reminded me that in some ways this phrase implies that somehow I received extraordinary grace versus the person I'm speaking of. I use it here, however, only to reference how easily I could have been in that person's place. In my case the expression should probably be "there but by dumb luck go I". It's so true. One turn in a different direction. One tragedy. One financial hit. We like to believe it could never happen to us. I met a woman once who changed my mind. Traci was happily married with two children. They had a lovely home. She was a stay-at-home mom, and her husband had a successful career. All was well in the world–or so she thought. One day, the checks started bouncing, and her life took a drastic turn for the worse. She discovered that her husband had a gambling problem. He had credit cards that were being sent to his work, and he was charging them up at an alarming rate. They were going to lose everything. She tried to hang in there and work things out, but the gambling didn't stop. Finally, she gave him the choice between gambling or his family, and unfortunately he chose the gambling. Imagine this: you have two kids, no husband, no house, no money, and no job (because you've been at home raising your children for the last ten years). Her life changed in the blink of an eye. At the time I met Traci, I was a stay-home mom with two kids and a husband with a good career. I felt connected to her. The next time I saw a woman standing on a corner with a sign, I looked at her differently. "There, but by the grace of God, go I," had a whole new meaning for me.

Since this is a book about hope, I'll tell you that the story doesn't end there. I met Traci through my connection with Habitat for Humanity. Most people know that Habitat partners with individuals to build a home. Many are surprised, however, to find out that they also come along side families and help them navigate through some of life's challenges. Traci was able to get some financial help so that she could go to school and eventually get a job. When she wasn't in school, Traci put in sweat equity on their new Habitat home. She has a good job, and her children have a warm, safe place to lay their heads at night so they can be rested for a good day at school. I've often wondered if the person who gave Traci a Habitat application realized she changed three lives that day. And so it goes. The needy become the needed. Traci is now a volunteer with Habitat for Humanity and speaks to large groups inspiring them to act. Her children are growing up in a secure environment with the opportunity to meet their full potential. Who knows what they will accomplish in their lifetimes because of a simple act of kindness and a set of hardworking volunteers.

These days, we seem to be living in the land of "me." What would I have done in that person's situation? How will this affect me? What does this have to do with me? This type of thinking separates us–isolates us, one from another. It stops us from simply walking up to someone and asking the question, "Can I help you?" or in the case of the one-legged kid, "Would you like to play?"

Let's talk about fun. Nursing home chair bowling–it's a blast. Once, our church canceled services for the weekend, and, instead, we went out into the community and served in a variety of ways. There were over a thousand of us digging ditches, feeding the homeless, putting AIDS kits together to send to Africa, and visiting nursing homes, among lots of other things. Our pastor called it Compassion Weekend. No sermon, no offering, no Sunday School. Just "be" the church in the world. Over time, this concept of compassion has become part of our culture at church, and is now integrated into all we do. One of the activities our volunteers do with seniors at the nursing homes is called chair bowling. You haven't lived until you've participated in this little diddy. Everyone gets in a circle in their wheelchairs (or stationary chairs), and a set of pins is positioned in the middle of the circle. A little ramp is placed beside the bowler. The bowler positions the ramp for maximum speed and accuracy, places the ball on top and *whoosh*, down it goes toward the pins. That's when the whooping and hollering begins. There's nothing more fun than a bunch of rowdy 90 year olds. One weekend, the volunteers and residents were having a great time bowling. Everyone was laughing and cheering for one another as they tried for strikes and spares. As the ramp was being moved, and the pins were reset, one of the volunteers noticed a woman sitting in the back quietly watching. She walked over, bent down next to the woman and asked, "Would you like to play?" "I'm lost," said the woman. "You're lost?" asked the volunteer. "I'm lost," repeated the women. As the volunteer looked into her eyes, she saw confusion–dementia. "I'm lost," the woman kept repeating, over and over again. I believe there are moments in our lives that define us. In that moment, the volunteer could have simply chalked it up to an elderly person with dementia and walked away. Some people may not have felt the effort worthwhile. This volunteer, however, chose compassion. "Why are you lost?" asked the volunteer. "They moved me here from a different place, and I'm lost." The woman was clearly distraught. The volunteer thought for a minute and said, "You're not lost. God knows exactly where you are right this minute. He's looking at you right now, and he loves you very much. You are not lost." What happened next had a huge impact on the life of the volunteer who shared this story with me. The woman lifted her head, and looked directly into the eyes of the volunteer. All of the fog and confusion completely cleared from her eyes. "I forgot about that," said the woman. "God does know where I am." Her voice was finally calm and clear. "I'm not lost," she said. Peace settled over her face. The tension left her body. The two sat together quietly for a few minutes, and then the woman said, "I'm lost." As quickly as it left, the confusion returned. But for that brief moment, there was a memory, an awareness, and a sense of peace. A gift had been given. That volunteer will tell you today that she'd do the same a hundred times over. She had given the priceless gift of clarity and peace, if only for a moment.

Later, the volunteer found out that the woman had been moved to a facility about thirty minutes away from where she had been for many years. Her son had visited her regularly in the old facility, but felt the drive was now too long, and no longer visited her. How do you tell a mother that her son won't drive thirty minutes to see her? She thought she was lost because no one came to see her anymore. Was it better to think he couldn't find her than he wouldn't come? I don't have the answer to that question. I will say, though, that a new relationship was formed that day. The volunteer now visits the woman, and a group goes once a month to paint fingernails, read novels, and enjoy a happy game of chair bowling.

I wonder how many seniors sit in nursing homes unvisited. It disturbs me to think about it. They've given us so much. They've risked their lives in wars, participated in the civil rights movement, invented things, and created the communities we now enjoy. They have so much to share. These people are our history, filled with stories and life-lessons. Can I make a recommendation? Go make an eighty-year old friend. It's time well spent outside the land of me.

A woman on the street, a man in the apple section of the grocery store, an old woman hunched in a wheelchair–all foreigners to our land. We make assumptions about them. We create barriers between *us* and *them*. We assume that *their* situation must fit into the neat little box that's filled with our own personal set of experiences, because, of course, everyone thinks exactly the same way we do in the land of me. It's about fear. It's about selfishness. It's about ambivalence. Remove those barriers, and we free ourselves to become participants in life rather than observers. When we open our minds to the possibilities–the possibility that someone might not be who we think they are, or the possibility that we can have a positive impact on someone's life–we begin to leave the land of me, and the world begins to change.

One Little Thing

For Compassion Weekend, myself and several others, volunteered to be Area Leaders. This meant that we were in charge of all the serving opportunities happening in a particular city, and we had sub-leaders working with us who were in charge of specific projects. After Compassion Weekend many people emailed or wrote to us to let us know what happened with their projects, and some contacted us later to let us know that they had established on-going relationships with the people they served. This letter was one of the latter.

"Dear Friend,

Thank you for introducing me to Franklin House. Had it not been for Compassion Weekend, I would not have become involved with the wonderful people there. I feel truly blessed. I am sending several pictures from the evening that Santa came to visit. I loved the excitement and energy of the evening so much. The plan was for them to enjoy a sing-along and then Santa and his helper would arrive. I was asked to take a picture of each of the residents as they sat on Santa's lap. By the way, this gentleman, whose mother-in-law used to be a resident, was the BEST Santa I've ever seen. Well, I so enjoyed the intimate moments that the men and women were having with Santa, that those are my favorite shots. The director also asked us to visit a couple people who were too ill to come to the party, and that was the most touching moment for me. The oldest resident was over 100 years old, and yet he still wanted to sit on Santa's lap and have a chat. What a blessing. Thank you for pointing me in that direction.

Vicky"

Chapter 3

The Drop Becomes a Ripple

Three years, eight months, and twenty days. For those who survived the killing fields it seemed to go on forever. I know a man who survived the killing of 1.7 million Cambodians. He is an amazing man. His strong will and patient spirit helped him survive. He will tell you that he is here today because of the grace of God and because of a series of individuals who, at great personal risk and sacrifice in some cases, stepped outside their land for a moment to help him. His story is remarkable to me.

When the Khmer Rouge came into power in the 1970s, people all over Cambodia were forced to evacuate cities and march to the remote countryside. At the time, Darren was 15 years old and living with his father, pregnant mother, and two young sisters in Cambodia's capital, Phnom Penh. The family began their march, but people were hungry and dying. Dead bodies lay along the roadside as they walked for nearly a month. Once in the remote location assigned to them, his mother had a miscarriage and lost the baby. His father was ill from hunger and overwork. Darren was forced to work in the fields all day and attend political indoctrinations at night. At one point, he was tied upside down by his feet and left hanging overnight for addressing a Khmer chief by the name "teacher." He had forgotten that the word had been banned. They imprisoned him in a place where he watched his people led into the jungle to be beaten to death. When he realized this would be his fate too, he decided to escape. Darren knew that there was a lake at the edge of the camp, but Darren didn't know how to swim. Nevertheless, the lake would be his only means of escape. He walked into the lake until the water was over his head and then he blacked out. He was a Buddhist at the time, and he says he remembers thinking, "I will learn to swim in my next life." When he woke up, he was on the other side of the lake. To this day, Darren doesn't know how he got there.

It wasn't long, unfortunately, before he was captured again by Khmer Rouge troops, who buried him in the ground up to his neck and left him to die. Hungry and dehydrated after being buried for some time, Darren assumed this would be his end. Days later, however, an ex-Khmer Rouge soldier came by and–knowing he would be tortured and killed if he was caught helping Darren–dug him out. Darren gathered his strength and headed back to his parents' village. When he arrived, he learned that everyone in his family had perished except one sister.

By the time the Vietnamese troops drove out the Khmer Rouge in 1979, approximately 1.7 million Cambodians had been killed. Even after the Khmer Rouge left power, however, Cambodia was still a very dangerous place. People were trying to flee to refugee camps. Darren, now married to Christina and working in Phnom Penh, agreed one night to escort a friend's wife and children to a refugee camp on the Thailand border. He also took his sister Rina, hoping she would be safe there at the refugee camp. When they arrived, though, the Thai government accused him of being a Cambodian spy and refused to let him return home. With the help of a Cambodian smuggler, however, Darren was able to have his wife brought to him.

The family was eventually moved to a United Nations refugee camp where they joined a church run by missionaries and they became Christians. They lived there for five years, and they had two children. Finally, in 1989, with the help of some people from the U.S. Immigration Office, they were granted permission to come to America. They arrived in the U.S. that year.

Darren, moved by what he learned from the missionaries in Cambodia, and determined to make a better life for his family, was admitted to a Theological Institute to begin his training to become a pastor. He hoped one day to pastor a Cambodian congregation. At the time, he and his family were living in a rat-infested apartment and barely getting by on food stamps. In 1992, when Darren completed his studies, he and his family moved to an area where he could begin his career as a pastor. But life was still a challenge. Their first apartment was condemned, and the home into which they subsequently moved was in an area riddled with gangs and crime. They were, now with three children, once again living in fear. That's when Darren heard about Habitat for Humanity. He didn't believe it could be true at first, so he referred another family and watched as they built their new home. Shortly after that Darren applied for a house, and, within one month, their application was accepted and construction on the house began. With Habitat for Humanity, homeowners are required to put in 500 hours of sweat equity–300 hours on their own home and 200 hours to help another person build their home. Money is raised for the building materials and land, but the construction is done almost entirely with volunteer labor. Darren says he remembers feeling terribly guilty as he began putting in his sweat equity because many of the volunteers were senior citizens. In his culture, having seniors do any kind of work was considered disrespectful. Seniors should rest and be honored.

Soon, though, after working side by side with the volunteers, they all became family. The whole family put in sweat equity hours. Mom, Dad, and their oldest did the heavier work, while the two younger children painted. It wasn't long before their home was finished; they moved into their "dream home" right before Christmas. Later, Darren planted a beautiful pear tree and roses in the yard. He also put up a basketball hoop for his sons. His family was finally home.

In America, we often hear these stories, and we see them on television and in movies, but for some reason they don't seem real. Perhaps it is because places like Southeast Asia are too far away. Although the tragedies of 911 opened our eyes to some of the violence in the world, for many people the reality of terrorism still seems unimaginable somehow. It's hard to fathom that pain and suffering is, in fact, part of daily existence for many people in our world. When we reach out to those in need—the hungry, hurting, and terrorized—their lives are changed and the effect ripples out into the world. When Darren speaks of the ex-Khmer Rouge soldier who dug him out, the missionary at the refugee camp who told him about Jesus, and those blessed Habitat volunteers who—at age 70 or more in some cases—choose to swing a hammer every day, he says, "Those who cared for us have shown us by example how important it is that we love and care for each other—they taught me what it means to have a *servants heart*."

For many years, Darren worked for Associated Ministries, helping low-income families make a better future for their children, and now he works for Safe Streets teaching families how to stay safe in what can be a dangerous world. He is on the Board of Directors for Habitat for Humanity, and he returns every year to Cambodia to do missionary work. He formed a non-profit called ICOC that does amazing work in Cambodia. The first year, they dug a well and built a home for a woman with two paralyzed children, and a disabled husband. Another year, Darren built an elevated home for a woman who had been living under a tree in a village that sits in a flood zone. His children have been extremely successful in school, achieving scholarships for college. And his sister Rina is now living happily in California with her husband and four children. I wonder sometimes how many lives Darren has changed for the better; I imagine that the number has to be in the thousands. A hand once reached out to him and he took it. Now he spends his life reaching out to others.

This, to me, is agape love. What an amazing thing. I learned this term at Vacation Bible School when I was about ten years old. My favorite definition of agape love is "selfless, unconditional love of one person for another". Agape love is God-driven. I don't think, as humans, we are truly capable of expressing this kind of selfless love on our own. Our egos hate the idea of selflessness. What about me and mine? The world tells us it's about survival of the fittest. How can I take care of my own needs if I spend my time selflessly caring for others? And yet there are people in the world who are intimately familiar with this concept. In fact, can you imagine a world where agape love doesn't exist? It saddens me when people share that their only "God experience" involves fire, brimstone, and judgment without love. That's not the God I know. My God is the embodiment of agape love. He didn't come to earth in the form of a man (Christ) to condemn us, he came so that we might know him better, and to provide us with the perfect example of a selfless, loving servant – He came to save us from ourselves.

Beth Moore, in her book *The Fruit of the Spirit*, talks about the concept of resonance. I'd never heard this description before, and it fascinated me. Beth once sat down with a master pianist and had him explain the concept of resonance to her. Apparently, if you play the middle C on a piano, all the other Cs on the piano vibrate. In addition, any other note that harmonizes with the middle C vibrates as well, creating perfect harmony (and resonance) by striking that one note–little old middle C. This idea struck a chord with me (pardon the pun), because I realized that I can be middle C. In physics, we learn that every action has an equal and opposite reaction. So I play my note and that vibration, that kindness, resonates out into the world in perfect harmony and bounces back to me! What joy to do the little I can, knowing that my action impacts another, ripples out into the world, and returns again to me as joy.

Sometimes that joy arrives in an unexpected package. I met a boy once, named Elly who was from Uganda. I met him here in America, when he was 15 years old. His story is really a testimony to his mother. She was the note, and Elly and his sisters are the resonance. And let me tell you, it showed. Elly had a light about him–a strength and courage for such few years on this earth. I wondered from where that light emerged, and he graciously shared his story with me. Elly was from East Africa, where war and corruption were part of daily life. Parents that are able, send their children to boarding schools because every day children are kidnapped on their way to school, abused, and forced to fight in a war they cannot possibly understand. Elly and his sisters were in boarding school not far from home for this reason. While at boarding school they were often taught what was in the teacher's head, because books were scarce and curricula were few and far between. Additionally, even if someone was fortunate enough to graduate with a diploma, work was scarce. There were very few jobs, and people with jobs sometimes went months without being paid. Unfortunately, there was nothing anyone could do about the lack of educational materials, scarcity of jobs, and irregularity of pay. There were palms to grease and bribes to pay.

This corruption was a constant battle for Elly's parents, and they chose to speak out against it. When I met Elly, he talked about an expression we use in America. We refer to the "haves" and the "have-nots." He told me that we have no idea what this really means. In Africa, it was part of daily existence. The "haves" will always have in Africa, and the "have-nots" will always have not. Elly and his parents prayed for change. But in Uganda, it was dangerous to speak out and it was dangerous to fight for a better future for your children. One day, Elly's father was kidnapped, and Elly's mother began a dangerous search for her husband. She went quietly from town to town gathering information, trying to find him. Each time she would get near to where she heard he was, he would be moved again. Finally, she heard he had been imprisoned in a neighboring city. After several days of traveling, she arrived only to find out he had been executed the day before. Grief-stricken and angry beyond comprehension, she vowed to provide a better, safer life for her children. This would not be the end of her story.

Elly's mother saved every penny she earned and sold everything she could while still keeping the kids in school, and, when she finally had enough money, she traveled to America. She had no family or friends here, but she knew how to work. Friends back in Africa kept the kids safe, while she worked two and sometimes three jobs, saving money to fly her children to America. Finally, after nearly a year, she had enough money for the tickets. She contacted a Ugandan travel agent and arranged to have the tickets waiting at the airport for her six children. On the scheduled day of departure, one by one, the children arrived at the airport, escorted separately by family friends for their safety because part of the group that killed her husband was still looking for the family. The children stepped up to the counter, however, to find that there were no tickets because the travel agent had stolen all the money. Back they went to school. "Can you imagine?" Elly said to me. "When does a person give up? When does a person say I can't do it anymore?" His mother, who had been listening quietly from the kitchen as Elly and I talked that day finally spoke up. "Never." She said.

On her knees in prayer that night she cried, then once again she worked. One of her jobs was caring for the elderly. A woman who worked with her there was named Maryanne. Elly's mother hadn't worked there very long, and didn't share much information because she was still afraid for her children and she didn't know who to trust. But she decided one day to share her story with Maryanne. Her decision was fortuitous because Maryanne, as many of us would be, was incensed and was moved to take action. Maryanne thought, "How could one woman go through so much and still have faith? How could she lose so much, and just get up the next morning and start all over again?" Maryanne believed that her persistence was a testament to a mother's love. Consequently, Maryanne got on the phone and began calling everyone she knew to help raise money for those plane tickets. Friends, co-workers, family, volunteer organizations—she called them all. Within a short time, the money Maryanne collected, combined with the new money Elly's mother had raised, provided her with enough money to purchase airline tickets for her children. This time purchase of the tickets was arranged by one of the leaders of a local non-profit in America. And this time, the children were safely placed on an airplane. Elly talked about the awe and wonder of coming to America. Everything was so different here. But he also spoke to me (at age 15) about freedom and power. As arrangements were being made for the tickets, Elly's mother was making arrangements for her children, applying for scholarships and grants so they could get a good education. When I met Elly, he was attending a private Christian school on scholarship and receiving outstanding marks. He spoke at a fundraiser one morning–close to 400 people were in the room and you could have heard a pin drop. We were enthralled. He spoke about how giving up individual parts of ourselves was necessary to build a future of which we can be proud. He said he spoke for minorities and young people who deserve an education and a future. He asked for an opportunity to make the world better for future generations. He challenged us to demand a world where children are protected in the moments when they cannot protect themselves. He spoke of his mother's love, prayers, and sacrifice and of her commitment to a life of security and dignity for her children. And he spoke of Maryanne, and other volunteers who changed the path of his life. There wasn't a dry eye in the house.

When Elly finished speaking that day a city official approached him, shook his hand, and asked for a signed copy of his speech. I'm certain she was thinking what everyone else in the room was thinking. This young man will change the world. A board member of the college he hoped to one day attend was also in the room. She too approached Elly and told him to call her when he was ready for college. This boy could write his own ticket. Several years have passed since that breakfast. I spoke to Elly's mother recently and she told me that Elly will graduate from college this year in civil engineering. His potential seems unlimited. It's hard for me to imagine that light of his hidden, or even worse extinguished, on the other side of an ocean. I do believe his mother would have found a way to get her children here eventually. But Maryanne played her note, and a chain of events resonated all the way to Africa and back. Although it may have happened otherwise eventually, that gesture of kindness provided salve to a tortured heart. A glimmer of faith in humanity was restored. And it doesn't end with Elly. His sisters became nurses, businesswomen, and mothers to a new generation–hands and feet to Elly's dream.

So when you say, "Who am I to change the world?" Perhaps the answer is, "I am a worker in a retirement home," or maybe, "I am only a volunteer." Even if you say, "I once was homeless," can you change the world? The answer is a resounding "yes!"

Five Little Things

1. Do a Neighborhood Food Drive.
Call or visit your local food bank and get a list of things they need. Deliver empty grocery bags in your neighborhood with a note attached requesting help and listing the specific needs of the food bank. Mention the date you will return to pick up the bags. A woman in our community did this and showed up at the food bank with 890 lbs of food one week after she dropped the bags off!

2. Make Someone Smile.
Try to make at least one person smile today just by smiling at them, making eye contact, or complimenting them.

3. Give Someone the Gift of Warmth.
Purchase a below-zero sleeping bag and drop it off somewhere where you know there are homeless people. You could end up saving a life.

4. Umbrella Anyone?
During the winter months go buy 5 or 6 umbrellas at the dollar store and leave them sitting at bus stops. Attach a note that says "Finders Keepers!"

5. Pay the Toll.
The next time you go through a tollbooth, pay the toll for the person behind you.

The Drop Becomes a Ripple

Chapter 4

--- ❋ ---

Even I

One day, a man was walking along the beach when he noticed a boy picking something up and gently throwing it into the ocean. Approaching the boy, he asked, "What are you doing?" The youth replied, "Throwing starfish back into the ocean. The surf is up and the tide is going out. If I don't throw them back they'll die." "Son," the man said, "Don't you realize there are miles and miles of beach and hundreds of starfish? You can't make a difference!" After listening politely, the boy bent down, picked up another starfish, and threw it back into the surf. Then, smiling at the man, he said, "I made a difference for that one."

I find this modern-day parable written by Laura Eisley so applicable. I think we all have moments when someone tells us—or we tell ourselves—that our actions don't count. We're one of so many people on the planet—a veritable drop in the bucket of humanity. I have to constantly remind myself that the drop becomes a ripple. Anyone can make a ripple, even the people we least expect.

Thaddeus was a perfect example. "Let us practice here on earth the things that matter in heaven." It was printed on the man's shirt. Grey scraggly hair, matted beard, brown teeth with hollows in between, standing on a corner holding a sign that read: "Hungry, God Bless You." Before Heidi's experience at the Dream Center, her thought process in these situations was painfully similar to mine. "Let's see, I need laundry soap, a gift certificate for my nephew, stamps at the post office... Oh my gosh, I'm stopped right next to a homeless person! What if he makes eye contact with me? Oh well, he probably makes plenty of money, and I'm sure he got himself into this situation. Maybe he just doesn't want the responsibility of a house or job. Turn green! Turn green! Well, I do have a granola bar. Maybe I should give it to him. Oh, he probably wouldn't want it anyway. He probably wants money for cigarettes, drugs, or alcohol. Why doesn't this light turn green!" She slides her hand over to lock the doors. Click. Finally, the light turns green, and she's on her way.

Heidi signed up to volunteer one day, at the Dream Center. The Dream Center is an organization that feeds and cares for homeless people. It was a crisp, autumn morning filled with the promise of a productive day. As they gathered at the center that morning, a man stepped forward to share the story of a homeless person he knew named Thaddeus. Apparently, Thaddeus had been almost completely blind for years. The Dream Center began by getting him food stamps; Thaddeus hadn't realized he qualified for them as a veteran. Then, they were able to get a local surgeon to perform eye surgery (for free) to remove his cataracts, which restored his vision. He was also offered a place to live and a new beginning, but chose to remain on the streets. In gratitude to those who helped him, he now volunteers every Saturday at the Dream Center.

Heidi wondered why anyone would choose to stay on the streets, but assumed her eyes were about to be opened. She was right. Heidi and her daughter Jessica, plus the other volunteers, spent the morning making hundreds of sandwiches to deliver that afternoon. Making preparations for a day of serving is always such a happy time in the volunteer process. There's something about working side by side with others for a good cause that feeds the soul. It doesn't matter whether you're digging a ditch or making sandwiches, the activity connects us by common purpose. Heidi and Jessica chatted the morning away, having a wonderful time. Once they were finished, they and a group of volunteers hopped in the car with a Dream Center leader to begin delivering the sandwiches.

Their first stop was an old run down motel near the edge of the forest. They were told to knock on each door and say "Dream Center. Would you like a sandwich?" Heidi wondered if the people knew they were coming. The whole prospect of this was a little bit scary. Her daughter was there with her. It's a fine line we walk as parents, precariously balancing between securing our children's safety and exposing them to what can be a pretty scary world. On the other hand, how can we teach our children empathy and help them to understand love and human kindness without exposing them to it? With one eye on her daughter, the first person Heidi met was Dottie. Dottie and her husband have lived in and run the old motel for 36 years, ministering to the people who live there. "What a sweet couple," thought Heidi. She handed them a sandwich, which they readily declined, saying, "There must be someone else that could use a sandwich more." They told her the Dream Center had just brought them a sandwich the day before. Heidi could tell by looking at them that they needed it. As they traveled from room to room, heads popped out, doors opened, as people gratefully received their sandwiches.

They piled back into the car, but didn't get far before they saw a homeless man standing on a corner. There stood scruffy Thaddeus holding his sign. "You have to meet this man," said the driver. So they pulled over and got out of the car. Heidi wasn't sure what to expect. Will he be safe? Will his speech be slurred? Will he be aggressive or scary in any way? Within seconds, any preconceived notions of who Thaddeus might be melted away. They ended up talking to him for quite a while. Heidi was amazed at how kind and gentle he was. She learned that Thaddeus loves to talk. He shared a story she will never forget.

Thaddeus told them about the time he traded his below-zero sleeping bag for a thin blanket because the other person needed it more. But the next week, he got a call about his daughter and had to go to Ohio where it was very cold. He really could have used that sleeping bag. When he arrived, he was walking down the street and found a below-zero sleeping bag still in the package tossed under the bridge. He knew God put it there for him. He gives God credit every day. He said that he is the weakest man he knows, but only for God's grace is he not using heroine anymore. Everyday he wakes up in the woods, tired and sore, but thanks his creator for another day to live and wonders what God would do with him that day. Thaddeus calls himself an "urban camper." He shared that even though he was offered a place to live, he chooses to stay in the woods so that he can help other homeless people. He feels it's his mission, and he wants to do everything he can for them. He said he doesn't need much to live on, so if he gets a lot of money in one day, he just smiles, knowing that God is going to show him later for what purpose or for whom the money is to go. He helps the Dream Center locate the homeless, and assists them with communications because he "understands the homeless perspective." What an amazing human being. We all could learn from Thaddeus. Heidi reached down to humbly shake his hand and thank him for his time. The day had been so much more than she ever expected.

Whose life do you think was changed that day, Thaddeus' or Heidi's? So many times, I set out to serve with what seem like selfless expectations. I want to go out into the community, into the world, making life a little easier for those I serve. My heart is in the right place, my actions

45

useful and needed. What ends up happening, however, is the complete opposite. I am the one who ends up being blessed. Yes, I clean the boxes out of Martha's garage, or weed Mr. Harrington's garden, but when I go inside to have some iced tea, there's a present waiting there for me. Not a present in the traditional sense, but a gift of love, of friendship, of connection. Even when the people I serve are hurting and unable to respond in a certain way, the gift is still there, waiting to be unwrapped. It's important to understand that sometimes the present is the reciprocal gift of presence.

In my years with Habitat, I learned that the Bible says not to charge interest when you loan money to the poor. Most major world religions agree on this principle. It helps me to apply this concept to the gift of time. If I give my time to the poor, the lonely, or the suffering, and if I give it hoping for a specific response, it is equivalent to charging interest for my time. We cannot serve with expectations. When our motives are misplaced, we are oftentimes disappointed in the result, and we miss the experience entirely. Where did we get the idea that a gift (time, love, compassion) won't cost us something? That's why it is called a sacrifice. We won't always know the outcome of our actions either. Why do we need to know? Does the gift become any less valuable? I hope one day to have enough spiritual discernment to find the entirety of the gift in the giving itself. Colossians 1:29 says, "To this end I labor, struggling with all His energy, which so powerfully works in me." Did you notice that it says His energy? God's energy, not mine. God's outcome, not mine.

Sometimes God's plan is a little different than our own. When I was a little girl, my mother became very ill. I knew she was sick, but had no idea how sick. Just before I turned six she died of breast cancer. Dead. What does that mean to a six-year-old? I remember asking my grief-stricken father all kinds of questions like, "What will they do with her body?" and "What does the inside of a coffin look like?" All the while wondering what kind of cookies she and I might bake together the next day. Summer came in waves that year with fits and starts. I didn't know what the future held for me. Promises were there for something new, something different. But then there'd be the whisper of her in the rustle of another mother's skirt, or her scent in a crowd, lingering for a moment, then gone as quickly as the thought itself. I remember hiding in the middle of the laundry hanging on the lines at my grandmother's house, fabric swinging softly in the summer wind. Touching sheets and aprons and socks. Wanting her.

Wondering if my mother's hands had once touched that place, and feeling like somehow if I could just touch the things that she had touched I could capture a piece of her and keep it. It took me quite some time to grasp the concept that she wasn't actually coming back. Those years were a struggle at times, but along the way, there were people who left their "land" to come into mine, or invited me into theirs. One of them was Mrs. Mauer. Her son Ronnie Mauer (it cracks me up to call him Ronnie as he is now RON–very grown up and masculine) was one of my good pals throughout childhood. He and I were in the same class all through elementary school. Ronnie had two sisters and two very busy parents who were teachers, community volunteers, coaches, and so much more. But no matter how busy she was, Mrs. Mauer never seemed to forget about me. In early elementary school, there always seemed to be a mother-daughter tea, or a parent-child activity night filled predominately with mothers and their kids. For most children, these events were a cause for excitement. For me, however, they were a stressful time, wondering if I would be able to find someone to take me when my father was busy or working. I would spend the weeks before making up stories about how I would probably be busy that night with one fun activity or another and wouldn't be able to attend. Looking back, I'm not sure why I bothered because somewhere in the back of my mind I knew I would always get a call from Mrs. Mauer. Without exception, several days before these events, my phone would ring. The conversation would go something like this: "Hello Kathy, this is Mrs. Mauer. I wanted to call and ask you a favor. Ronnie is going to the parent-child activity night with his dad, and the girls are going with their friends. I don't have anyone to go with, and I am so disappointed. Would you consider maybe going with me?" With great excitement, I would agree and the two of us would have a fun-filled night together. I didn't realize until probably high school what she had done for me, and, not until I had children of my own, did I consider the sacrifice. What a selfless act of kindness and an amazing example to a child of agape love. I'll carry it with me always.

I often think of my father during those times. I can't even imagine what it was like for him, having to tell my brother and I that our mother was gone, while dealing with his own pain and sadness. There was a hole in our house and in our hearts. His work was stressful, and now he was left alone to raise my brother and I. Little by little, I suppose in search of something to numb the pain of loss, he became an alcoholic. Several years after my mom died, he remarried. As an adult, I can look back at that time and imagine how difficult it must have been for my new mother, moving into a home with a widower and two children whose mother had died. As someone once said, "The house was devoid of her presence, yet filled with her absence." Bless her heart, she has been a good mother, and is still hanging in there with us today, after all these years. And I'm proud to say that my father hasn't had a drink in close to twenty years. Not long ago, he shared with me that the last time he got drunk was in a bar outside the hospital where I was having surgery at age 25. We were waiting for test results to come back for possible breast cancer. (The tissue came back healthy.) I've never asked him, but I bet there was some negotiating going on with God, in the bar that night.

With a lot of prayer, and the support of AA and the 12-step program, my father is still sober today. One of the things I've learned in many years of volunteer work, and from talking to people about AA, is that sometimes the only one who can help us, is someone who's been there. They know how you feel. They've lived it. Each of us has something to contribute based on his or her, own life experience. My father is a living testament to that 12th step. AA isn't always the answer, but for those who go through the program and actually complete the 12th and final step (carrying this message to others–helping and supporting other people), the success rate increases exponentially. Statistics show that those who go on to sponsor people who are new to the program and help them stay on track, have a much higher success rate in staying sober themselves. Many times, I've watched the process of someone taking the focus off of their own struggles and placing that attention on another, both people finding their way back. We sometimes get so caught up in our own weakness or misfortune that we assume we have nothing to offer. It's easy to give that which comes naturally and effortlessly to us, but to dig deep into the darkness and offer up our true selves, chinks and all, is the ultimate gift. We must remember that we cannot disconnect our history from our destiny. They are intrinsically connected.

My dad is a great example of this. It hasn't been easy. He still attends AA meetings, struggles with depression, and lives with a shunt in his head from a fall and resulting brain injury a few years ago. Yet when he was able to, I would find him delivering meals on wheels to shut-ins, walking next door to the elementary school to help children with their reading, and speaking at AA meetings. And those are the people he barely knows. I have pictures of that 6'3" man sitting at a miniature table with my daisy-picking daughter, surrounded by teddy bears having a tea party. Life is what you make of it.

Even I

One Little Thing

This e-mail was sent by a man who wanted to share that he's started thinking about love in a new way.

"Dear Friend,

I had a chance to serve this past week. I was driving down the freeway and saw someone up ahead trying to fix a tire. It was raining and I thought to myself "Stop! Try to do something–hold an umbrella at least. That's what we're called to do." (So many times I have just driven by in a hurry trying to get where I was going.) I got out of my car, and held the umbrella over the man. He spoke only broken English. The spare was flat and the pump leaked air. I found out he lived in Kent, and we were in Fife, which was about a half hour drive (not that that was going to make a differenced in what I was about to do). He called his wife, and then I told him to get in my van and I would take him home. He couldn't believe it. He was worried his pants would get my seat dirty. "Come on, get in, it's o.k.," I said. I knew the dirt would wash out. That wasn't going to stop me from taking him home. We talked on the way, and he goes to a Spanish speaking Assembly of God church in Seattle. He was able to communicate that serving others is what church is all about. As I dropped him at his front door he said, "God bless you," and I returned the greeting. As I left I realized God had blessed me, and God had blessed him through me. Good stuff.

P.S. This is not shared to bring glory to me, but glory to our God who is in control of everything.

Dale"

Even I

Chapter 5

❀

I'll Take Red

Hope. It can at times, take unimaginable courage and strength. Whether one is battling a severe illness or dealing with death, divorce, or financial or other of life stresses, it's easy to begin sinking into hopelessness–especially when that hope is misplaced. That painful thing, whatever it may be, begins to take over. I was surprised to find, however, both in doing my research and in meeting people who've experienced this, that hope–and health–can prevail. I'm not a doctor, and I'm certainly not an expert in this area, but I found an overwhelming amount of research that shows that when we take the attention off of our own troubles, illnesses, and pain, and begin focusing it unconditionally on another hurting or needy soul, we ourselves begin to heal. In addition to physical healing, emotional and spiritual healing seem to come as well.

In articles written by the Corporation for National and Community Service, researchers including Graffe, Luks, Payne, and Hemphill stated that "volunteering can improve self-esteem, reduce heart rates and blood pressure, increase endorphin production, enhance the immune system, buffer the impact of stress, and combat social isolation." In addition, their medical and scientific documentation supports that "volunteering results in a heightened sense of well being, improves insomnia, and hastens surgery recovery times." Researchers attribute this, in part, to the fact that volunteers are put into highly social situations, which increases their opportunity for close personal relationships. That, in turn, strengthens their sense of identity. In fact, the Public Health Agency of Canada stated that "volunteer work improves the well being of individual volunteers because it enhances social support networks." People with strong social support networks have lower premature death rates, less heart disease, and fewer health risk factors over all. All that from gathering with friends to rake someone's yard! It's really pretty amazing. I've been fascinated to meet people who have experienced this first hand. One of them was named Jennifer.

When I first met Jennifer, she was going through what so many others have experienced–a painful divorce. Her whole life had been turned upside down. She had two boys counting on her, and she had to start all over again. She shared that in this situation, it's easy to become completely absorbed in the pain of it all. The hurts seem unbearable. How do you move forward? It feels like being in quicksand, stuck and sinking. Jennifer realized that she needed to somehow pull herself out. She thought that maybe if she could just take the focus off of herself for a day or two, she might begin to heal. So she called the church and signed up to do a compassion project. "I'll go wherever you send me," she said that day. They signed her up to paint fingernails at a retirement home called the St. Frances House. It was Veterans Day, and she was told to look for someone there named Lonnie (the lead volunteer that day). Lonnie turned out to be this big, burly guy about 6'4" tall, maybe 250 lbs with a buzz cut so flat and tight, it looked like you could balance your soda on it. "He looked intimidating to say the least," said Jennifer. When she saw Lonnie, Jennifer felt her stomach clinch. In her world, big burly men were not physically violent necessarily, just scary. Looking at him brought back all the pain and anxiety she'd been feeling–until he opened his book. It was a book of poetry he had written himself. He opened his mouth that day and what came out was such a surprise to her, such a gift. His voice was gentle sweet, and kind. His poetry was beautiful. Softly, Lonnie read to an enthralled and grateful group that day. And Jennifer painted fingernails. She thought she was going there to serve, and ended up being served herself in so many ways. Her anxiety melted away, and her fear was replaced with a hope for something more, something different. She told me that her entire image of what a man is was changed that day.

Jennifer laughs, when she talks about the time she now spends every month at the St. Frances House. "Most of the residents have Alzheimer's, so they can't even remember who you are!" says Jennifer. "It's so humbling. You might have painted Margaret's fingernails five times in the last six months, and each time she will say, 'I haven't had my fingernails painted in years! Do you have red?' And then Margaret will say, 'What is your name darling?'" Yet Jennifer feels she is the one who's blessed with every visit. "To hold their hand, touch them, listen to them–that is what matters," she told me.

The process of serving has healed her heart. I was excited to hear that Jennifer hopes to one day start an outreach for parents of struggling teens. She's been through some challenges with her boys as they were growing up and wants to provide support for other parents experiencing some of the same difficulties. Jennifer's goal is to unite parents and churches of all denominations to pray for these kids and provide a solid support network. "All it took was that first act of service," says Jennifer. "It changed the path of my life from darkness and despair to healing and hope. It helped me find my purpose."

Sometimes when we serve, it feels like we should be thanking the person we serve, not the other way around. Serving others is an opportunity they have given us to physically express the love of God. The Bible says that God *is* love. And His love is unconditional in a way we can scarcely understand. He doesn't love us because we are cute or especially loveable. He doesn't love us because He needs our love. He created us so that we could have a relationship with Him. He loves us beyond measure because He *is* love itself. If God is love, and we are created in His image, aren't we called to *be* love? For me, there is a great freedom in yielding to that call. To release the responsibility for outcomes and just do what I am called to do. And if I know that what I'm doing right now isn't positive, I can start fresh with a new purpose–not tomorrow, not in an hour, right now-this very minute. Why not? There's a wisdom in recognizing that time is not an unlimited resource. We shouldn't gamble with it. We're all scared at times, and none of us has all the answers. But when we feel God calling us to do something, we oftentimes, in our weakness, say, "I cannot." We need to remember that God says, "But you can. I will equip you to do it." And there will be times when the task seems daunting.

Tina lived in a broken down trailer in a mobile home park on the outskirts of town. The black mold had gotten so bad she had to tape off her bedroom because of the smell. Her closet was literally a tent outside. And rain poured in through the light fixtures inside her house dripping into the buckets below. Her six grandchildren slept wherever they could find a spot, while Tina and her daughters dished up their next serving of methamphetamine. When Rick (from the Dream Center) first stopped by with sandwiches, there were hundreds of tiny holes all over the kitchen floor. He asked one of the girls how they got there, and she told him that her mother and boyfriend were so high on meth one night that they thought the kitchen floor was covered with spiders and spent hours stabbing the floor with a kitchen knife. One of Tina's daughters had gotten out, and gotten clean, but the family was a mess, and the children, their mothers, and grandmother all needed help. Sometimes, we are called to love those who may seem unlovable.

55

The first thing Rick did was feed everyone and pray for them. He noticed that Tina could hardly walk and found out she had knee cancer. He asked if he could pray for her knee and was surprised when she said yes. He contacted different organizations to help with the kids, the house, and the drug situation. Every day or two, someone from the Dream Center would go and take more sandwiches. A few weeks after the first visit, Rick went back and was shocked to see Tina up walking around. He asked her what happened. She said she had been to the doctor, and her knee was completely healed. The cancer was gone. She cried and said it was a miracle from God. The family was getting help, and she was struggling to get off meth. The first time I heard about Tina was when a firefighter friend got a group together to build a shed for her. She was working hard to make things better, and they wanted to give her a clean, dry place to put her things. When the group finished with the shed, it was so much nicer than her trailer, she started sleeping in it. Thanksgiving came, and the Dream Center brought the family a basket filled with food. Tina and her family were so touched by everything that had been done for them, that they carried that food into the woods nearby and fed the homeless families living in tents there.

Even with the positive changes she made, life still wasn't easy for Tina. Months later, she came to Rick crying, saying she couldn't continue under her own strength anymore. Rick sat with her for a while, and this time Tina did the praying, finally giving control of her life to God. Tina's life may always be a struggle in some ways, but she knows now that she isn't alone. Three generations have been changed. Her daughters are now clean, and their children are on a great path. The girls work at the Dream Center, and one of them has a new baby. "I watch her with her child," Rick shared with me. "She's the most amazing, gentle, loving mother. How does that happen? Where does that sense of love and nurturing come from when all you've been exposed to is drugs and pain? It can only be God," he said. Tina spends her free time feeding the homeless, and she is better each day from the inside out. She has good and bad days, and she does what she can to help restore a sense of normalcy and dignity in the lives others by sharing her own struggles.

Dignity is an interesting thing. I used to think it couldn't be taken from you, but I realize now it can. Sometimes people reach the point where they just give up. Their dignity gets stripped away by life, other people, or sometimes by their own actions. But dignity can also be restored. It can be given to someone, not by working for them, but by standing next to them and doing the work together. Sometimes all it takes is an ally to just be there beside them. Not hovering over them, hands on hips and filled with judgment, but standing side-by-side as equals. Sometimes, even positioned down below, giving a boost up. I remember a volunteer telling me once that he, and a group of people, were digging a drainage ditch for someone's house. They had been there most of the day, and the homeowner, a hardworking single mom, had been there next to them digging as well. Sometime in the afternoon, he looked up from the ditch and saw the woman sitting on the edge, head in hands. She must be exhausted, he thought, and took some water over to her. He sat beside her and asked if she was o.k. At first she couldn't speak, but finally, through a tear-stained face, she choked the words out. "Why did you come?" she asked. "I have never done anything for you. I have nothing to give you. You don't even know me, and yet you're here, working in the hot sun all day for someone you've never met. I don't understand." He sat next to her and explained that he felt blessed by doing what he could to help her. This was a way for him to show her that God loves her. He was the one receiving the blessing. He told me that this interaction saddened him in a way. Have we become such an isolated people that selfless acts of kindness are incomprehensible? What has happened to us? There was a time when simple acts of kindness were the norm, not the exception. Look at the example of Christ's life here on earth. He didn't care about power or status. You would find him amongst the people, feeding the hungry, healing the sick, caring for the poor. His companions were fishermen, laborers, and even prostitutes. He didn't isolate himself from them because of who he was. He loved them. When the disciples surrounding him said he was too busy to spend some time with the children, he said, "Let the children come to me." What a perfect example to us. We are all loved and valued equally by God, regardless of that which might make us appear to be "less than."

This was the example Dan built his life on. "You can only invite stinky people," he told his small group one night. They had been talking about this process of being like Christ, loving people unconditionally through our actions. There were some chuckles, and jokes about who would clean the couch and carpet. But Dan wasn't kidding. He wanted to form a small group where they could invite homeless people to come spend time with them and form relationships. He thought about it, prayed about it for months, but time and work got the best of him, and it never seemed to happen. Then Dan landed in the emergency room with pancreatitis. I didn't know anything about this disease, but apparently it can be deadly. In his case, the inflammation was the width of his fist and about 18 inches long. The pain was excruciating. "It comes and goes, but when it comes," he said, "the pain is so horrible, you wish you were dead." He'd been sitting in the emergency room, and all of a sudden it hit with such force, he collapsed on the floor, doubled over in agony. He remembers two things from that night. One was a man behind him saying, "This is ridiculous! Somebody needs to help him." The other was a nurse that came. As he lay on the floor, he looked down a hallway and saw a tall, heavy-set nurse dressed in an old-fashioned type of nursing outfit. She didn't have the little hat on, but he remembers thinking her outfit was strange. She approached him, bent down, put her hand on him and said, "You are going to be all right. Someone will be here soon." Then he watched her walk down the hall, open a door at the end of the hall, and go in. That was when he blacked out. Dan was in a coma for a week. The problem wasn't curable. Yes, there were temporary fixes. He could walk around the rest of his life with a bag attached, but his activities would be very limited. They gave him a 20% chance of living. Dan said he had lots of time to reflect in the hospital. "Why can't you just take me!" he begged God. "I don't want to live my life this way." The days passed by, and through it all, Dan kept thinking about the homeless. He felt God prompting him to do something, and for every excuse Dan came up with God had an answer. Each time an answer came, he said he would hear a voice in his head say, "What are you going to do now Jonah?" He chuckled when he told me this story. "Apparently God has a sense of humor," he said. Jonah is a book in the Bible about a man who tested God's patience. Dan always had an excuse. "I don't have the money, so I need to sell our rental." This was his first excuse. The next day someone called his wife and said they had driven by a property they owned. They were able to find his contact information on the county assessors website. They said they knew it wasn't up for sale, but it was exactly what they had been looking for and were wondering if they might be willing to sell it. "What are you going to do now Jonah?" There it was again. "I've completely lost my mind," he thought.

Then there was his health. As Dan's strength improved he was able to go home and wait for the next surgery. Again his thoughts turned to the homeless, but he thought it wasn't possible. How could he help others when he was in such poor physical condition? He hadn't had the surgery yet that required the bag, but it seemed unavoidable. The final appointment was scheduled, but when he went in, he learned that they had lost his records. When the records were found, he went back into the doctor's office, and when they did the scan, all signs of pancreatitis were gone. Vanished. Dan believes his healing was a miracle. He would be able to go back to work. "But what about the homeless?" He thought.

Then the headaches and memory problems began. Dan later found out that the drugs they used when he was in a coma had caused some damage. He was unable to go back to work. The doctors tried different drugs and eventually they came up with a combination that allowed him to function in the world with minimal pain and complications. He would never, however, be able to return to his old job. Fortunately, he had good disability insurance, which would completely cover him for the rest of his life. This time when he heard God say, "So what are you going to do now Jonah?" Dan had an answer.

A meeting had been called to set up a Freezing Nights program. This is an organization that monitors the weather, and when the temperature drops below the freezing mark, they take a van around and pick up all the homeless people in the area. Different churches volunteer their buildings to house the homeless for the night. Cots are set up, and volunteers provide dinner, snacks, breakfast, and a lunch to take with them the next day. At first, Dan was hesitant to step forward and lead, but once he did, two other people immediately said they would help him. He was able to use his work experience at Boeing to set up an entire set of procedures to run this program. "When we first started, there would be one person sleeping and five people watching (security)," Dan told me. "But it wasn't long before there would be thirty people sleeping and one watching." There are always plenty of volunteers there, but many sleep in the other room while the homeless sleep, too. Many of the volunteers have formed relationships with the homeless people they serve. Dan has given each of them a nickname. They sit for hours and play board games and chat together. "And boy can the room get ripe!" he told me. "I prayed for stinky people, and they came." Dan did share with me that most homeless people take great pride in staying clean. They use public bathrooms to bathe and rinse their clothes, but it's difficult to do it all the time when you are living on the streets. Some freezing nights facilities have washers and dryers, so volunteers are able to wash at least one outfit for each person that night.

Dan feels he can relate to these people. Many of them are disabled like he is. "These people need to build new memories," he told me. "The old ones hurt too much." He is helping them to do this. One of the men called "Old Al" is trying to get up the courage to call his daughter. He wasn't there for her growing up and worries she would reject him now. Dan is helping him through this process and will be there with him when he reaches the point where he feels he can make that call. They had a Christmas party this year and Harlan (a volunteer) played Santa. "We wanted a big, rough, burly Santa, not a wimpy one!" said Dan. So many tears were shed that night as each person received four gifts. The gifts were personal things, special to them as individuals. "Gifts were given to us as well," said Dan. The homeless would dig into their bag and pull out something so special and priceless and give it to one of the volunteers. New memories, relationships, and trust are being built. Dan now misses his friends during the warmer seasons. He drives his van around to find them, chat, and have a meal together. Recently, as he was driving around visiting people, he decided to stop by the emergency room where he had collapsed. He had always been curious about that nurse. The first thing he did was try to find that hallway with the door at the end. When he found the spot where he had collapsed in the emergency room, he looked down and could see the hallway and door. Dan walked down the hallway, opened the door, and, to his surprise, the room was a chapel. One way in, and one way out. That's odd, he thought. Why would a nurse walk out of a chapel, straight down the hall to him, put her hand on him, say something, then walk back down the hall and right back into the chapel without saying anything to anyone else? The next thing he did was ask about the nurse. He described her in detail, including her personal appearance and her attire. He learned that there had never been a nurse working in the ER that fit that description, and there was certainly never one wearing that outfit. Dan feels he had an angel watching over him that day. He hadn't yet found his purpose, and apparently death was not an option.

Because of everything he's been through, Dan now understands that sense of "community" we all need. We were made for it. We give our children a time-out by themselves when they misbehave. In our prison system, we use solitary confinement as a means of severe punishment. When we're angry with a spouse, we might not speak to them for a little while. Those things get our attention because we weren't made to be isolated from one another. This need for community applies to all of us–even those (such as the homeless) who seem to be standing in another land.

When Dan looks back at his own life, at the ups-and-downs of his personal relationships, and at all the health issues he had to go through, he's finding clarity now as he begins to see how it all comes together. The "big picture" seems to be unfolding before his eyes. Each thing seemed to happen for a reason, and each incident took him one step closer to his purpose. Little by little, he found that as he took his focus off of his day-to-day life, his financial stresses, his illness, and disability, and began to direct his attention toward others, he began to heal—not only physically, but emotionally and spiritually. None of those challenges was a picnic, but the lessons he learned—about himself and others—have changed his life and the hundreds of lives he's touched.

I'll Take Red

Five Little Things

1. Bake it up.
Many people aren't able to bake anymore because of physical limitations. Bake some cookies and deliver them to a home-bound neighbor or senior.

2. Happy Birthday, Baby!
When women escape domestic violence situations, quite often they and their children leave with only the clothes on their backs. Children's birthdays can be forgotten or put off. Assemble birthday (goodie) bags and donate them to a women's shelter.

3. Knit One, Pearl One.
I have a friend who knits hats whenever she is watching TV. Learn to knit, and donate the hats to people in need.

4. Become a Pen Pal.
Although it's a blessing to serve in foreign countries helping with things like irrigation systems, building, and providing food and health care, it can also be difficult being away from friends and family. Write a letter to a missionary in a foreign country. You can get names and addresses from your local church.

5. Go on Litter Patrol.
Sometimes we forget that each of us is responsible to help care for our earth. Pick up some litter the next time you go on a walk.

Chapter 6

―――― ✿ ――――

Give Me Five!

Remember Flat Stanley? Years ago in elementary school, we made this little flat guy out of paper named Stanley and mailed him to someone. That person would take Stanley on an adventure, take a picture of Stanley in action, and then mail him to someone else. ("Stanley visiting the world's largest ball of string," "Stanley at Aunt Bitsy's house on Thanksgiving," "Stanley on a camping trip.") Eventually, Stanley would make his way around what seemed like "the world" and, at the end of the year, get sent back to us! Growing up in a small town, it seemed so exciting to see all the places Stanley had visited! It was so simple–a little flat guy, a letter, a postage stamp, and *bon voyage*, Stanley!

I got to thinking about Stanley recently because of $5.00. Not long ago, we did an experiment at church. Every person in the congregation was given a $5.00 bill. The idea was to take that $5.00 and do something kind for someone else with it. It was so interesting to see the different things people came up with. Apparently, a few people returned the $5.00 saying they waited and waited for an opportunity to do something kind with it, and nothing came up. Others took that $5.00 and added to it in order to do more. One family of three, for example, took their $15.00 ($5.00 each) and matched it with their own $15.00. They took that $30.00 and purchased 5 ducks for a family in Uganda. Those ducks would provide protein-enriched eggs for the family to eat and sell for profit. Another woman had a co-worker who was recently divorced. She was barely getting by each month. The woman had mentioned that she had to give up her Sonicare toothbrush in the divorce. This may seem like such a trivial thing to many of us, but it wasn't to her. She had been left with almost nothing. The church member took the $5.00, added the money necessary to buy a Sonicare toothbrush, and purchased it for the woman. She put it in a plain paper bag with the woman's name on it, and put it in the lunchroom at work. Later, the woman came by in tears to tell her co-worker what had happened. She couldn't believe it and was trying to figure out who would do such a kind thing for her. She said she would never forget it. This (secret) act of love brought the giver such joy, that she later sent each member of her own family $5.00 in envelopes, requesting that they use it to do something kind for someone in their community. Not long after, anonymous kindnesses started popping up in California and Montana... just like Flat Stanley!

In addition to the $5.00, people were given little red paper hearts each week. You could take as many as you wanted. The idea was to continue doing acts of love in the community and write down what you did on your paper heart. The only stipulation was that you couldn't put your name on it. Each week, the hearts were turned in as people came to church. By the end of the month, thousands of paper hearts covered a huge wall in the sanctuary. As we came in, we could stand and read what was written on the hearts. One of my favorite parts of this experiment was to see what the children had done.

One parent of a young child said she spent some time in the car, talking to her kids about "compassion" and what it means. She asked them to think about this and try to come up with ways they could show love and compassion to others. One of her (elementary-aged) girls was gearing up for the Washington Assessment of Student Learning (WASL). This is a huge test in the State of Washington that determines how the students (and schools) are doing academically. Students spend quite a bit of time preparing to take this test, and it can be very stressful. On the first day of WASL testing, the girl created little notes for everyone in her class that said the following:

> *Three tips for WASL:*
> 1. *You have learned everything you need to know.*
> 2. *Do your best and you will be your best.*
> 3. *You are AMAZING!!*

She went in early and put them on the desks before everyone arrived. The response was overwhelming. That thoughtful little act lightened things up and created excitement in the classroom on what could have been a very anxious day for many.

One teacher shared the following example of a child's act of compassion:

> *I teach second grade in the public schools. Last week one of my "brightest" was stymied by untied shoelaces. Seeing this as a clear safety hazard, I asked him to tie his shoes, but he*

didn't know how! One of my struggling students volunteered to help him tie, and smiled up at me as she did it saying, "I'm really good at tying shoes." I told her what a nice thing it was that she did, and explained that it was an "act of compassion." Later in the same day, the shoes were untied again, but this time two children were helping, and they happily declared, "We are doing acts of compassion!"

As teachers, parents, grandparents, aunts, uncles, or even friends or leaders of children, we have a responsibility to "do as we say." Many of us profess goodness and compassion to the children in our lives, but as a parent, I've discovered that my children pay a lot more attention to my actions than my words. As adults, we have the capacity to plant seeds of hope and compassion so that our children, and even their children, can grow up understanding what it means to consider another person's needs without judgment. I remember meeting a man at Habitat who helped open my eyes to this concept. I was in my twenties at the time, and I hadn't really thought much about words versus actions, or more importantly, that people can show God's love and compassion without ever opening their mouths. The man I met was partnering with Habitat to build a new house for his family. He was Ukrainian, and he had a very thick accent. He wanted to talk to me about the "preachers" at the job site. I asked him what he meant, because I didn't know of any pastors that were working at the job site that day. He told me that the volunteers were preachers. I explained that I knew all the volunteers at the job site that day, and none of them were preachers. I began to assume we were having issues with a language barrier, when his son came over and offered to translate. Patiently, the man explained (as his son interpreted for me) that although the volunteers may not be the pastor of a church, they were the "real" preachers. They preached without ever saying a word. They preached with their hands, their backs, their hearts—compassion in action. I was humbled, to say the least. As a young person, this lesson was life-changing for me.

It isn't easy being a parent these days. The world seems to be moving so fast. It starts out the same. Our children come into the world the same way they always have—innocent, unjaded, full of all the potential in the world. But today, the world is so full of cynicism and people seem to have a never-ending need for "more." Our children are exposed (bombarded, really) at such an early age to a world that wants things bigger, newer, better, and they want it now. And they can get it now. We have instant food, instant messaging, and instant information. How often do we go to the library anymore? Our children watch us work hard to get more, but then the world tells us there's more to get, so we work harder to get more, and so on, and so on. As a nation, we seem to be running on empty. We get stuff to try and fill up some unseen hole, but it never seems to be enough. It just leaves us emptier... joy deferred. We complain about what we don't have rather than using what we do. I've come to the conclusion that all the "stuff" in the world will never be enough. We need to teach our children the notions of plentitude and purpose.

There's this amazing place in Mexico called Rancho Sordo Mudo. It's a free boarding school for deaf children. In Mexico, they don't have special education like we do here in the states, so deaf children either don't attend school at all, or they go to school and have no means of understanding what the teacher is saying. Several children at the ranch were simply abandoned on the streets of Mexico because their parents didn't know what to do with them. When the children arrive at Rancho Sordo, most of the time, they have no formal language. They've developed means of communicating with their families by pointing, and pantomime. When they arrive at the ranch, they're given the gift of sign language. Children come to the ranch as early as five years old, and they can attend until they are 18. It's the most amazing environment. The children are nurtured, taught, and parented, as if by their own parents for nine months of each year. They are given an amazing education and a strong spiritual foundation, while also meeting their physical and emotional needs with vitamins, exercise, doctor's check-ups, nutritious food, even vacations, and lots of love and hugs to go around. The children are so full of joy! It's been an incredible experience taking our children down there each year to serve for a week. The team going to Rancho Sordo Mudo normally has one large project to work on while there, such as putting a new roof on, sheet rocking classrooms, or painting. We work hard during the day, but we get to eat all our meals with the kids, and late-afternoons and evenings, we can spend time playing with them.

I remember playing with the kids one afternoon, after a hard day's work. Our son Coleton was about 12 or 13 at the time and had spent the whole day climbing up in the rafters of a building we were working on and stringing electrical cable. He was the only one small enough to shimmy around up there, and I'm sure it was more than 100 degrees in the rafters.

He was hot, tired, and ready for some down time. Now Coleton is my electronics kid. Given the opportunity, he would be "plugged-in" at all times. He would have loved nothing more than to whip out the old Nintendo DS and share a game with one of the kids at the school, but we had other plans. We spent the entire afternoon catching lizards. One of the kids would take a broomstick and lift the ivy, and all the kids would laugh as these beautiful lizards came running out from underneath. We would scramble to catch one as they scurried across the hot pavement. Once a lizard was caught, we'd all gather around and decide what name to give it. When the kids at the ranch get to know you, they give you a sign name based on your interests, looks, or personality. It ends up being one sign, rather than having to finger spell each person's name. We did this for the lizards. After we had named and admired the lizard, we would release it back into the ivy and begin the hunt for another one.

After almost a week of working, eating, and playing with the kids, not only were Coleton's sign language skills unbelievable (so good, in fact, that he was interpreting for the adults), but he wasn't the least bit interested in turning on the Nintendo DS. Toward the end of the trip, our leader Greg asked Coleton if he would be willing to lead our morning devotions. Coleton said he would, and he began to think about a topic. I didn't ask him about it over the next day or two as he prepared, but as a mother, I was wondering if he would be ready, and I was curious what the subject of his talk would be. He was ready. Coleton talked about the challenges and sacrifices of Abraham and tied his talk to the challenging lives of the kids who attend school at Rancho Sordo Mudo. He spoke of their parents' sacrificing time with them, so that the children might have a better life. He talked about faith, unselfishness, and hanging in there when hope seems futile. Coleton began to cry. There were twenty-three people listening, and twenty-three people were crying. Out of the mouths of babes...

These kinds of experiences are life-changing for children. I wish every child could have the opportunity to see the world through someone else's eyes. Through witnessing and participating in unselfish acts of humanity, they learn kindness, humility, and commitment—*the gleaning of goodness.*

Many years ago, farmers would cut their fields at the end of a growing season. The wheat would then be bundled in preparation for sale and consumption. Afterward, small bits of wheat would be scattered across the land, left over from the gathering process. The owners of the land could have raked up the bits in order to use every part of their crop, but most didn't. It was customary to leave behind those parts for the less fortunate to gather as a source of food. This gathering process was called "gleaning." Just as the hungry gleaned the fields for food, our children glean bits of understanding as they witness acts of compassion—nourishment for the soul. We need to feed our children.

Rick from the Dream Center shared a story with me once, of a little girl who desperately needed this type of nourishment. Her mother had been severely physically and sexually abused as a child and had been a drug addict for many years. Her motel room was one of Rick's stops. The Dream Center is often referred to as "the church that never sleeps," and it's so true. Many times, Rick knocked on that door, and many times, the little girl's mom wouldn't answer. Finally one day, as Rick made his rounds and knocked at the door once more, a tiny face appeared. This was the face of sweet little Sara. Rick brought sandwiches each time, and eventually they invited him to come in. He asked if he could pray for them, and when he did, Sara's mom cried. She said it was hard for her to believe that there could be a "good" God in the world with all that she had been through. After several visits, though, she asked if he would take Sara to Sunday-School. Rick was thrilled. Some volunteers at the Dream Center picked up Sara the following Sunday, and they headed off to church. Sara was in heaven. She was like a sponge each week, soaking it all up. She was laughing, playing with the other children, and participating in every activity she could. Each week she would go home and share what she'd learned with her mother, and Rick could see that light began to slowly overtake the darkness. I don't know what happened with Sara and her mom, but I do know that Sara's mother was finally exposed to a different kind of human connection—one that doesn't hurt.

Maya Angelou says "Good done anywhere is good done everywhere." I love that. I've heard the difference between kindness and goodness described in this way. "Kindness is the feeling that's in your heart, and goodness is the doing of the kindness." When one (in kindness) performs an act of goodness for another, it changes everything. It transfers the kindness from you to them. In this case, a bit of kindness is deposited into the heart of a child. And like any deposit, there will be interest earned. That is the "good done everywhere." That kindness, if nurtured will grow and result in new acts of goodness, fueled by God, and fulfilled, in this case, by a beautiful little girl named Sara.

Children can do amazing things. I attended a meeting recently at my kid's school where we were discussing possible outreach events. One of the options intrigued me, so I spent some time learning about it. The organization is called "Hoops of Hope," and apparently it was started by a nine-year- old boy who had heard about the plight of hundreds of thousands of orphaned children in Zambia, Africa. His name is Austin, and he was so moved by the thought of what it must feel like for those kids to lose their parents, that he wanted to do something about it. So in 2004, he started by shooting baskets in his driveway to raise money. I've heard that Hoops of Hope is now the largest free-throw marathon in the world. "Similar to a walk-a-thon, participants raise awareness and funds for children who have been orphaned by HIV/AIDS by shooting free throws." As of 2009 nearly 50% of Zambians are under the age of 15–orphaned by this horrific disease. As a matter of fact, every 14 seconds a child loses a parent to AIDS. The nation of Zambia has been ravaged. But Austin, age 14 as I write this book, is making a difference there. His website says that; "Money raised this year by Hoops of Hope will be used to build a medical clinic in Chilala, Zambia, provide 450 bicycles and 750 mosquito nets for AIDS caregivers in Sinazongwe, Zambia. It will build dormitories for the Jonathan Sim Legacy School in Twachiyanda, Zambia, and finance ten care centers in Swaziland." Kids across the nation are catching Austin's passion. In an interview posted on his website, Austin said, "Given the opportunity, kids will blow you away." He's absolutely right.

Regardless of whether we are parents or not, the children of this world are watching us. They look at pictures of us in magazines and newspapers. They listen to us on the radio and watch our actions on television. They notice how we behave in the line at the grocery store and how we do (or don't') let someone merge as we drive down the freeway. The children of this world are paying attention. As adults we have a moral responsibility to them–just as the generation before had a moral responsibility to us. Arthur Dobrin wrote, "Whatever good there is in the world, I inherit from the courage and work of those who went before me. I, in turn, have a responsibility to make things better for those who will inherit the world from me." Children are only children for a short time. It's our responsibility to love them, to find a way to connect with them, and then lead them (by example) toward an understanding of goodness, purpose, and humanity.

One Little Thing

Many times at church, group projects are offered, or people come up with their own individual projects with friends or family. The following is an e-mail shared by Martha, a woman who is a faithful member and volunteer in our church. It's one of my favorite e-mails because it demonstrates that acts of kindness don't have to be monumental (or expensive) to have an impact. It also demonstrates what most of us will have to work a lifetime to achieve—the purity of a true servant heart. The spelling may not be perfect but the intent is.

"Dear Friends,

I looked forward to giving out cookies, People do not know what to think about getting something free, with noning in return. We keep getting ask why are we doing this, we would say to show we care about you, and give you a blessing. The skate boader's real like geting the cookies. There keep coming back for more, and real enjoy them. My Team prayed for the rain to stay away until we was done with the give away, well we got all back in are car's, and rain start up at that time. We went form 10.00 to about 2.15. So cool to how God bless us that day.

Your Sister in Christ,
Martha"

Give Me Five!

Chapter 7

_____ ❀ _____

Finders Keepers

"Is _this_ all there is?" Do you ever feel that way? As kids, we used the expression, "Finders keepers, losers weepers." I can remember tormenting my brother with that one. "Sorry you left your $5.00 bill right there where anyone could take it. Finders keepers!" Poor guy didn't stand a chance with me around. I found all kinds of great things (including blackmail material like naked baby pictures). You never knew when some girl might come over. Now that I have children of my own, I have to laugh when I hear my daughter yell, "Finders keepers!" as she comes running down the hall, older brother close behind. Lately though, I've been thinking about finders keepers in a different way.

Over the years I've had a variety of different jobs. Some of them felt meaningful–like I was making people's lives a little better in some way– and others seemed sort of silly at the time. Later, however, I looked back and realized I had learned something while I was there, something I was able to use later in life. Have you ever had the experience where you knew you were doing exactly what you should be doing? You realized that the task precisely fit your abilities, and you knew you'd found your purpose? Many people fail to experience that phenomenon because of fear and, perhaps to a certain extent, laziness. It can take a lot of prayer, and some searching to get there. Many times, we find our purpose in unexpected places. At one point in my life (I can't remember exactly when), it occurred to me that if I just let go of control and began doing what I knew was right– perhaps turn down the "road not taken"–I'd somehow find my way. That's exactly what has happened. Volunteering is a great way to get there. You can experiment with different things in order to find that one thing, that thing that separates you from everyone else. And when you find it, there's such a sense of peace. You were made for that thing. You found it and you get to keep it! (And you didn't even have to embarrass anybody with a nude baby picture.) But there's a catch. You can't find your purpose by doing nothing. Sometimes it means doing something in the evening when you are tired after a long day's work. Sometimes it means a few hours on a weekend. But isn't it worth it? I can't imagine anyone would want to come to the end of their days asking, "Is this all there is?" I don't want to feel that way. I want to come to the end of my life sliding into home, full blast, belly down, mud flying, grit between my teeth because of the smile on my face, hands stretched toward home. I want to hear "Well done!" I want to know that I made the most of every single day, and that I made use of the gifts God gave me. What does making the most of our lives entail? It means getting up off of our butts and doing something about it. Rob, a youth pastor I know, says, "Don't let your *but* get in the way." *But* I don't have the time... *But* I don't have the money... *But* I have too many problems of my own to take care of.

Mohatma Gandhi said, "The best way to find yourself is to lose yourself in the service of others." Carol Wells Reed was lost in a pile of children one day. Little ones draped across her shoulders at each side, one on each knee, one sprawled across her lap, one flopped over her head–all of them not wanting to miss one word or one picture in the story book she was reading to the children that day. Carol was sitting on the floor at the Gene Tone School for homeless kids. Each morning, the bus would drive through the streets of Tacoma, stopping at underpasses, bus lines, shelters–anywhere you might find a homeless child. Once the children arrived at the school, they were given backpacks filled with school supplies, and toiletries. They were also given clothes and food. When their basic human needs were met, they were given an education. Sometimes, the kids came for three days, sometimes three months, but all of the children were loved and cared for at the Gene Tone School. Carol was a volunteer. In her life, she had been Mother, Secretary, Banker, Kitchen Designer, and so much more. Her volunteer work at the school, however, began to define her in a way that no career ever had. She had children drawn in around her, touching her cheeks, arms, hair–more than anything, just craving human contact. As she sat Indian style that day filled with joy beyond measure, she realized she'd found her purpose. She started by getting her employer involved in a book drive. The next year she asked for clothing and toiletries, and she collected 100 items. Each year, the number of items grew. On the tenth year, they collected 50,000 items. Later, she joined the Lions club and started collecting school supplies for homeless and low-income children in her local school district as well. It wasn't long before she realized that so many items were being donated they had a storage problem. The school district suggested she start a much-needed clothing bank.

As she began to research the plight of homelessness and very low-income children, she started to understand the positive impact you can have on a child by providing some very basic things that their parents might not be in a position to offer. Most children don't want to stand out–they simply want to fit in. They want to be on an equal playing field with their peers. Studies show that if you can embrace children when they are little and meet their basic needs by spending some time with them, reading to them, listening to them, and supplying them with simple items like decent clothing, you can change their image of themselves. These children tend to stay in school and out of mischief.

This was the beginning of what is now "Lions For Kids."

It started with a little, old house donated by an individual, and with the help of many volunteers and donors, Carol turned it into a beautiful little boutique where each child felt catered to as they picked out their free clothing, toiletries and school supplies. Lions For Kids opened their doors in 2006 and had 650 visits that year (each child can come once a month). In the 2008 school year, they had 1,685 visits. Now, the doors are open at their new facility, completely renovated with donated materials and volunteer labor. The centerpiece of this gorgeous facility is a "serenity garden." According to Carol, "Many of these kids live in unimaginable chaos and have never had the pleasure of smelling a rose, lavender or lilacs. The serenity garden is a kid-friendly, aromatic, tactile place with pathways, water features, bird feeders, hiding places, and other wonders enabling each child to have a place to 'just be' for a time once a month." So many of these children are constantly being uprooted and have to leave anything that's "theirs" behind. Because of this, when the children go in, they are also allowed to select books, videos, games, and toys so that they have something tangible and fun that they can call their own. Lions For Kids has grown to so much more than its humble beginnings. Through dedication, and lots of encouragement from others, what started with a heap of children and a loving heart has now has grown to an organization that compassionately serves thousands of children each year. Carol didn't just dream about what could be. She didn't let her "but" get in the way.

I've heard it called paralysis by analysis. Sometimes, we think too much and feel too little. It's important to learn to be still, to pray, and to be reflective. Many times, if we sit still long enough, God will provide us with the answers. But then what? What good is enlightenment, if you don't act upon it in some way? There needs to be a transition from prayer to action. Sometimes, all it takes is a little encouragement.

I learned recently that (believe it or not) the goose has something to teach us about encouragement. Sometimes, I find myself distracted by odd things. My mind begins to wander off as I notice things that might normally go unnoticed. One day I was watching a flock of geese fly by and I began to wonder why they fly in a V formation. I decided to look it up on the internet. I found out all kinds of interesting things about geese. Did you know that when geese flap their wings, it creates an updraft for the bird immediately following? By flying in a V formation, the whole flock adds at least 71% greater flying range than if each bird flew on its own. Also, when the lead goose gets tired, he rotates to the back, and another goose takes over. Another thing that made me curious was why they honk all the time while they're flying. I found out that they honk from behind to encourage those up front to keep up their speed. And finally, I learned that when a goose gets sick or is wounded and falls out of formation, two other geese fall out of the formation and follow the injured one down to help and protect him. They stay with him until he is either able to fly or until he is dead. Then they launch out with another formation to catch up with their group. Who knew the goose had so much to teach us about compassion, community, and encouragement.

We need each other. One of the organizations I work with in my job is called Love In the Name of Christ (Love INC). Love INC is a non-profit that helps churches help their neighbors in need. I spoke with Judy who works at Love INC in Pierce County to better understand how their system works. Calls come into community churches every day from people who are homeless and hungry—people who are out of work and need a little help with a utility bill to get them through to the next month. Love INC helps by screening the calls that come in and then either providing referrals to local resources that are available or collecting a little bit of money from several neighborhood churches in order to meet the need of the individual. But it's not just about resources or money. One of the reasons I love this organization is that it provides a vehicle for the unification of the body of Christ. It hurts me to think that sometimes the world sees Christians as divided by denomination. Yes, we do have areas of theological disagreement, but I believe most of us would agree that we are called to be faithful in caring for the sick, the poor, and the hurting. Love INC is about coming together for one cause: to serve others. This practice has changed the impression of those they serve. Those in need see the churches in our community as unified, not separate. I love looking at my spreadsheets each month showing unification in action. Need: Bob Smith (married, 3 children), needs $217 help with electric bill shut off date: next week–out of work). Action: received pledges of $75 Baptist Church, $25 Presbyterian Church, $17 Catholic Church, $50 Methodist Church, $50 Non-Denominational Community Church. Need met. With Love INC, the calls go out: "Who has firewood? Who has clothes? Who can provide funds for this or that?" And then the calls come in: "I have firewood." "I have clothes." "I can help financially." We've all heard the expression. "I don't care what you show me, until you show me that you care." Judy says, "Sometimes we have to do the practical to get to the spiritual."

Spiritual or not, I am addicted to National Public Radio. My kids hate it. "Oh Mom, not the BBC again!" I have my favorites, but every once in a while a story comes on that moves me. My favorite stories are the ones where a person uses their gifts or talents to help others. Recently, I was listening to an interview with an organization called The Kitegang, a non-profit toy company. I'm not sure if it was the creator or a leader of Kitegang who was being interviewed, but he was talking about the beautiful kites they design and build all over the world. Apparently, not only do they help the economy in underdeveloped areas by manufacturing kites and other toys–providing people with work and an income–but they also take kites into slums and refugee camps and teach people how to fly them. According to the interview, while working for the UN, Kitegang founder Patrick McGrann saw that in addition to needing jobs, people (children and adults) in war-torn and poor areas of the world also need to have fun.

After listening to their story on the radio, I looked up their website www.kitegang.org to get more information. The website said that one of the areas they serve is along the Chad-Sudan border where Kitegang serves as an outreach for "children fleeing the horrors of Darfur." If you've done any reading on the atrocities these people have experienced, you will understand that they have been traumatized beyond our comprehension. Kitegang goes into the camps and helps children (and adults) build, decorate, and fly their own kites. Not only does it give them a bit of fun, but they have found that there are "psycho-social healing possibilities" as well. One of the things that fascinated me during the interview on the BBC was listening to him talk about the kids needing to take out their anger and aggression on the wind. He explained that the wind is strong in many places they go, and they make the kites durable so that teenage boys can tug and pull and run and even slam the kites into the ground–angry at the world for what's been done to them. But eventually they tire–having released some of that anger out into the wind– and are able then to laugh for a moment and enjoy the magic of it all. And I can just imagine the little ones, faces all lit up like Christmas, waiting their turn to guide something beautiful up into the air and make it fly–pure joy. We have been given life. It's our gift (and responsibility) to live it!

As I think about those children flying kites in Africa, I am reminded of an invitation we received one night to go to a local fire station. A friend of ours who's a firefighter/medic with my husband had gone on a trip to Guatemala and wanted to share a slideshow of his trip. I remember being incredibly moved by the photos of children literally living in the dumps there. There were photos of cardboard houses and men with machine guns riding on the back of soda trucks. It was a completely different world than I had ever seen. Paul had gone down there on a medical mission trip with "Healing the Children" after Guatemala's civil war ended (which destroyed much of the nation's economy). While he was down there, he rode along with a fire company that ran many calls each day. Most of the calls were the result of violence, with lots of shootings, stabbings, and crashes. He talked about how shocked he was at their lack of equipment and training. "They didn't have ambulances. The *Bomberos* (volunteer firefighters) would respond to these calls, grab the patients from the streets, and throw them in the back of a pickup truck. They just transported; they didn't provide a whole lot of care." Paul witnessed several people die in the back of those pickup trucks and knew he needed to do something to help. He went back to his hotel that night trying to think of how he could teach them to make better use of their limited resources. Over the next few days, with the help of a 12-year-old interpreter, Paul taught about a hundred students techniques in basic bleeding control with cut up hotel bed sheets and cardboard boxes to use for splints.

Paul returned each year, which turned into several times a year, to train and provide supplies to the *Bomberos* of Guatemala. He started the BRAVE Foundation (*Bomberos* Resourceful and Valiant Efforts) to provide emergency response training and equipment to volunteer firefighters there. In 2007, he was granted a leave of absence from the fire department so that he could move down there and volunteer full-time. As of the last time we spoke with Paul, the BRAVE Foundation had organized the delivery of 20 firefighting vehicles and more than $1 million worth of medical and rescue equipment since its inception. What's more, the BRAVE Foundation has begun construction on a new fire station in San Juan la Laguna "The concrete structure was poured bucket by bucket, and local school children were given the day off from school to each carry a bucket of rocks from the lake shore to the construction site for the concrete mix." More than 1000 Bomberos in Guatemala have now received EMT training because of the BRAVE Foundation's efforts. Recently, Paul moved out to the country to help an indigenous Mayan community. The needs are huge there, and if you can imagine, they have never had anyone to call when there was an injury or accident because nobody was available to respond. Paul and his group are teaching the people of Guatemala that firefighters are here to help. Not long ago, we went out to dinner with Paul when he was back visiting for a couple weeks. He talked about how rustic it is in Guatemala and wished he had a paint ball gun to shoot the rooster that wakes him up every morning at 4AM. "I guess that wouldn't go over very well with the guy that owns the rooster though," Paul said. He brought a friend of his (one of the *Bomberos*) to dinner that night, and you could see how much respect Paul has for his peers there. "These guys are so poor and they try so hard. They have no other resources to make a program like this work on their own." Talk about one person making a difference. Craig and I are blessed to know him.

I believe that when we stop worrying about what the world tells us we should be doing, and begin to think about the things we love and areas where we're gifted, God will guide us to where we should be. Over and over again, I have experienced His provision. So many times I find myself wondering how we will manage this or that, only to be surprised, once again as our needs are met. We run a small food pantry out of a little garage at our church. One Thanksgiving, some volunteers were filling food baskets from the items we had in stock to give to low-income families. We had established set lists of items to place in each box, so that we could give the families items for breakfast, lunch, and dinner. Unfortunately, as the volunteers came to the last few boxes they realized they were short. One of the boxes needed pancake mix (we didn't have any), and we were completely out of eggs to place in the last few boxes. Shortly after the volunteers discovered they didn't have these items, Larry (who works in facilities) walked over to the food pantry with a large container of pancake mix and a bottle of syrup. Someone had donated those two things that morning at church, and he wanted to bring them over. Moments later, an elderly man pulled his car into the parking stall by the food pantry. He walked up, and in his hands were two 18-packs of eggs and $4 in cash. He proceeded to tell the volunteers that eggs were buy one get one free at the local supermarket! With those donations, they had exactly enough to fill every box. Coincidence? Someone once said, "Coincidences are miracles in which God prefers to remain anonymous." I don't believe in coincidence.

Five Little Things

1. Need a Ride?
There are many seniors and disabled people who either don't have a vehicle or are unable to drive. Offer to transport someone who can't drive to a doctor's appointment, shopping, or church.

2. Give Them a Rain Check.
I live in the Northwest, and it rains a lot here. Most of the time all of the shopping carts are soaking wet even if they have been brought in and placed under cover. Bring a towel and wipe the rainwater off of some shopping carts next time you go to the grocery store.

3. Thank You.
Sometimes we get busy and forget to thank people for the difference they made in our lives. It's easy to assume they already know. Write a thank you note to someone who has had a positive impact on your life.

4. Give Blood.
Blood banks become dangerously low during certain times of the year. Make a blood donation to the local blood bank, and while you're at it, see if you are a bone marrow donor match for someone in need.

5. Hit It Out Of The Park!
When you are on a tight budget, sometimes just having enough money to put food on the table can be a stretch. The extras aren't even a consideration. Give a pair of tickets to a baseball game or concert to a struggling single parent.

Chapter 8

❋

Are You My Neighbor?

As I occasionally grumble over empty pockets, a sore back, or incomplete chores at home due to a day of serving, I'm reminded of the single mother forced to move because she can't pay her rent, or the lonely senior with slippery steps starving for companionship. How could I possibly complain? Not long ago, we got a call at our senior outreach Laborers For Christ (LFC) for help on a mobile home. The owners needed gutters cleaned, windows washed, and their yard weeded. Upon further investigation, however, we learned that many homes in the same senior complex needed attention, so we decided it would be fun to turn the mobile home visit into a big work party.

A few days later, the happy sounds of weed-eaters being fired up, and anticipatory chatter of volunteers and their children, filled the air. As the work started on the 19 homes, heads began to peek out of doors, and before we knew it, the community was filled with volunteers and residents ages 9 to 90. Out of nowhere, lemonade and homemade "Grandma" cookies appeared, and someone made a big pot of coffee. We found out that one of the women had been caring for her sick husband for two years and had just attended his funeral that morning. Volunteers washed her windows and offered help with other things that had been neglected. Halfway through the second day, we discovered that one of the volunteers was a resident there. She had been asking the manager for two years for a list of people with needs in the community so she could serve them, but the residents wouldn't ask a neighbor for help. By the end of the day, she had scraped moss off decks, pressure-washed steps, and formed new relationships with many of her neighbors. Another resident was making plans to visit the woman who lost her husband and invite her to a Seniors Group. One woman (I would guess her to be late 80s) came out and gave the family who was working on her home a stack of beautiful home-made dish cloths she had knitted. I looked at the faces of the couple receiving the gift and would have sworn they had just been handed a million dollars. The gift was priceless. Even more families made plans to come back and continue the work, and more importantly, the relationships that had been formed that day. Time and again, the residents there expressed their amazement that families would give up their own personal time to come serve them, asking for nothing in return, and in addition to that, (thanks to this great guy I know named Rich who feeds people), serve them a delicious lunch. What the residents didn't realize was that in serving them, we (the volunteers) had been served. Luke 6:38 says, "Give, and it will be given to you. A good measure, pressed down, shaken together and running over, will be poured into your lap. For with the measure you use, it will be measured to you." I, in my ignorance, thought we were there to clean gutters. God, in His wisdom, had a much bigger plan. There I stood holding my teaspoon, while God poured out his love with a five-gallon bucket. Just as one candle may light a thousand, one small act of compassion grew into a multitude of blessings. One of my favorite Wikipedia definitions for compassion is this:

Compassion is a profound human emotion prompted by the pain of others. More vigorous than empathy, the feeling commonly gives rise to an active desire to alleviate another's suffering. It is often, though not inevitably, the key component in what manifests in the social context as altruism. In ethical terms, the various expressions down the ages of the so-called Golden Rule embody by implication the principle of compassion: Do to others what you would have them do to you. *Ranked a great virtue in numerous philosophies, compassion is considered in all the major religious traditions as among the greatest of virtues.*

And what Biblical reference do you suppose they are speaking of when they mention "all the major religious traditions" of this "great virtue?" Could it be this? "Love your neighbor as yourself." Many are familiar with this passage from the Bible, but some may not be familiar with the context or with the parable that follows it.

"Love your neighbor as yourself" was part of the Old Testament law, but the Jewish teachers had often interpreted "neighbor" to include *only people of their own nationality and religion*. Once, Jesus was speaking to a group of people including a Jewish "Teacher". Jesus was telling the group to "...love your neighbor as yourself". The Jewish "Teacher" then asked Jesus a question (about the greatest of the commandments). When he did this, he was trying to trip him up and justify himself. He wanted to see if

Jesus could qualify his interpretation. The teacher thought he could do this by asking, "…and who is my neighbor?" Jesus responded by telling him the Parable of the Good Samaritan. It went like this:

"On one occasion an expert in the law stood up to test Jesus. "Teacher," he asked, "what must I do to inherit eternal life?" "What is written in the Law?" he replied. "How do you read it?" He answered: "Love the Lord your God with all your heart and with all your soul and with all your strength and with all your mind; and, Love your neighbor as yourself." "You have answered correctly," Jesus replied. "Do this and you will live." But he wanted to justify himself, so he asked Jesus, "And who is my neighbor?" In reply Jesus said: "A man was going down from Jerusalem to Jericho, when he fell into the hands of robbers. They stripped him of his clothes, beat him and went away, leaving him half dead. A priest happened to be going down the same road, and when he saw the man, he passed by on the other side. So too, a Levite, when he came to the place and saw him, passed by on the other side. But a Samaritan, as he traveled, came where the man was; and when he saw him, he took pity on him. He went to him and bandaged his wounds, pouring on oil and wine. Then he put the man on his own donkey, took him to an inn and took care of him. The next day he took out two silver coins and gave them to the innkeeper. 'Look after him,' he said, 'and when I return, I will reimburse you for any extra expense you may have.' "Which of these three do you think was a neighbor to the man who fell into the hands of robbers?" The expert in the law replied, "The one who had mercy on him." Jesus told him, "Go and do likewise." (NIV, Luke 10:25-37)

To give you a little background, Samaria was a part of Palestine that had at one time been the capital of Israel. "In 721 B.C. it was captured by the Assyrians who deported much of the population and replaced them with foreign colonists. The colonists were pagans who eventually intermarried with the remaining Jews. They adopted the religion of Israel, but they also continued to worship their pagan idols." (Christian Bible Reference) The

Jewish people thought of the Samaritans as foreigners, religious heretics, and an inferior race. At one point, the Samaritans even offered to help them build a temple, but the Jews wanted no part of them. By the time Jesus was on the scene, the Jews had hated the Samaritans for several generations. The Christian Bible Reference Site (www.twopaths.com) gives this explanation: "With that background, it is easy to understand that there was no one the Jewish expert in the law would have considered to be less of a "neighbor" than a Samaritan. If a Samaritan man could be a "neighbor" to the Jewish man who was robbed and beaten, then the definition of "neighbor" would have to include *all* people, regardless of race, religion, nationality or any other artificial distinction. The Samaritan man gave freely of both his time and his money to help a Jewish man who was not only a stranger, but also was of a different religion, a foreigner and an enemy of his people. In His *Parable of the Good Samaritan*, Jesus challenges us to "Go and do likewise." We do not have to agree with other people's beliefs and opinions or condone their actions, but Jesus calls us to overcome our prejudices and show our kindness to *all* people of the world and consider them our "neighbors.""

When God looks at us, He sees us as neighbors to each other, not by physical proximity necessarily but rather by divine proximity (those who are placed in our paths). The trick is to look where we're going so that we don't accidentally pass right by our providential "neighbor" and keep on walking without ever noticing they were there. We need to pay attention.

Here's a story one of our pastors shared with us (which he found on the internet) that really exemplifies the power paying attention:

> *One day, when I was a freshman in high school, I saw a kid from my class walking home from school. His name was Kyle. It looked like he was carrying all of his books. I thought to myself, "Why would anyone bring home all his books on a Friday? He must really be a nerd. I had quite a weekend planned (parties and a football game with my friends in the morning), so I shrugged my shoulders and went on.*
>
> *As I was walking, I saw a bunch of kids running toward him. They ran at him, knocking all his books out of his arms and tripping him so he landed in the dirt. His glasses went flying, and I saw them land in the grass about ten feet from him. He looked up and I saw this terrible*

sadness in his eyes. My heart went out to him. So I jogged over to him, and as he crawled around looking for his glasses, I saw tears in his eyes. As I handed him his glasses, I said, "Those guys are jerks. They really should get lives." He looked at me and said, "Thanks!" There was a big smile on his face. It was one of those smiles that showed real gratitude. I helped him pick up his books, and asked him where he lived. As it turned out, he lived near me, so I asked him why I had never seen him before. He said he had gone to private school before now. I would have never hung out with a private school kid before. We talked all the way home, and I carried his books. He turned out to be a pretty cool guy. I asked him if he wanted to play football on Saturday with me and my friends. He said yes. We hung out all weekend and the more I got to know Kyle, the more I liked him. My friends thought the same.

Next Monday morning came, and there was Kyle with the huge stack of books again. I stopped him and said, "Boy, you are gonna build some serious muscles with this pile of books everyday!" He just laughed and handed me half the books. Over the next four years, Kyle and I became best friends. When we were seniors, we began to think about college. Kyle decided on Georgetown, and I was going to Duke. I knew that we would always be friends, that the miles would never be a problem. He was going to be a doctor, and I was going for business on a football scholarship. Kyle was valedictorian of our class. On Graduation day, I saw Kyle. He looked great. He was one of those guys who really found himself during high school. He filled out and actually looked good in glasses. He had more dates than I did and all the girls loved him! I could see that he was nervous about his speech. So, I smacked him on the back and said, "Hey, big guy, you'll do great!" He looked at me with one of those looks (the really grateful kind) and smiled. "Thanks," he said.

As he started his speech, he cleared his throat, and began. "Graduation is a time to thank those who helped you make it through those tough years, your parents, your teachers, your siblings, maybe a coach... but mostly your friends. I am here to tell all of you that being a friend to someone is the best gift you can give him or her. I am going to tell you a story." I just looked at my friend with disbelief as he told the story of the first day we met. He had planned to kill himself over the weekend. He talked of how he had cleaned out his locker so his mom wouldn't have to do it later and was carrying all his stuff home. He looked hard at me and gave me a little smile. "Thankfully, I was saved. My friend saved me from doing the unspeakable."

I heard the gasp go through the crowd as this handsome, popular boy told us all about his weakest moment. I saw his mom and dad looking at me smiling that same grateful smile. Not until that moment did I realize its depth. (Original Author John Schlatter- Internet Adaption, Author Unknown)

Never underestimate the power of your actions. With one small gesture you can change a person's life.

At yoga class one morning my friend (and instructor) Anne challenged us to ask ourselves a question. What if we thought to ourselves each morning, "Just for today..."? It occurred to me that the concept can be applied in a lot of different ways, including altruism. What if... just for today I helped someone with their books? What if... just for today I smiled at everyone I came in contact with? What if, just for today I thought about how my actions that day impacted the environment? What would happen? Maybe tomorrow, I would wake up again, and decide... What if... just for today? There are so many things in this life that we don't have any control over. The one thing we do, however, is the way we perceive, react, and interact with the world and the people in it–in short, our attitude and our actions. Sometimes when I find it difficult to peer outside the land of me, and I feel a good old-fashioned pity party coming on, I try to place myself in someone else's shoes. When I do this I realize that regardless of who or where I am in my life, I have something to offer. It's about gratitude. The following list of affirmations is a good reminder for us to appreciate what we have.

I am thankful:

For the wife who says it's hot dogs tonight because she is home with me and not out with someone else.

I am thankful for the husband who is on the sofa being a couch potato because he is home with me and not out at the bars

I am thankful for the teenager who is complaining about doing dishes because it means she is home, not on the streets.

I am thankful for the taxes I pay because it means I am employed

I am thankful for the mess to clean after a party because it means I have been surrounded by friends

I am thankful for the clothes that fit a little too snug because it means I have enough to eat.

I am thankful for my shadow that watches me work because it means I am out in the sunshine

I am thankful for a lawn that needs mowing, windows that need cleaning, and gutters that need fixing because it means I have a home.

I am thankful for all the complaining I hear about government because it means we have freedom of speech

I am thankful for the parking spot I find at the far end of the parking lot because it means I am capable of walking and have been blessed with transportation.

I am thankful for my huge heating bill because it means I am warm.

I am thankful for the lady behind me in church who sings off key because it means I can hear.

I am thankful for the pile of laundry and ironing because it means I have clothes to wear.

I am thankful for weariness and aching muscles at the end of the day because it means I have been capable of working hard.

I am thankful for the alarm that goes off in the early morning hours because it means I am alive. (Author Unknown)

In this economy, I am thankful for my job. A couple of years ago I was offered a position at our church. I was spending quite a bit of time down there because of our outreach to seniors, and when the Director of Benevolence decided to retire, I guess they thought I would be a good fit. It's been an amazing experience. In my job, I come in contact with all kinds of people on a daily basis, and the lessons I've learned have been tremendous. A while back, I coordinated a memorial for a beautiful young woman who had been shot in a drug deal gone bad. She had been struggling for years with drugs. With no family in the picture, her boyfriend (also shot but survived) was charged with the task of planning her funeral. I was surprised to hear he had been turned away by two different churches because of the circumstances of her death and his lack of faith in God. Aren't those the people we pray will show up at the church? He brought her picture in to me and I remember being struck by the beautiful woman before me with the most striking bright blue eyes I had ever seen.   I got together with him several times to make sure we included everything we could to honor her and commemorate her short life. I normally enjoy this part of my job, which probably sounds odd, but I feel like I am able to help people start the grieving process and organize all the little details that they never thought they would have to think about it. It gives me joy to bring them peace in this way, and walk with them through the process. Most of the time, memorials are a celebration of life and a transition from this earth to an eternity with our creator. But sometimes–once in a while–I find no hope. It's just plain sad.   This was one of those times.   As the day approached, I couldn't stop thinking about this young woman–about bad choices and dangerous friends, about her mother also dying at a young age. And as the day of the memorial arrived it only got worse, as one by one, friends showed up at the service, many of whom also seemed lost. The young man had told us that they weren't religious and that he didn't want the pastor to "preach" at them.   The pastor honored that. He had different people share their memories of her, and he spoke about friendship and "being there for each other." He did what they had agreed to, which was to pray for them at the beginning and end, and speak just for a moment about another kind of hope–one not found on this earth.   But as I looked around, I could see that his words were falling on deaf ears–one man even got up and walked out to the foyer, while others looked away. The pastor spoke, people shared, some nice music was played, and he closed in prayer. Just as the pastor opened his mouth to tell everyone where the reception was being held and to thank them for coming, an elderly woman sitting in one of the front rows stood up, turned around, looked at the group, and said, "I have something I want to say."

Now, I had noticed this woman arriving with her husband that day because they were quite a bit older than all the other guests. I wondered if they were grandparents to this young woman or the boyfriend left behind. All the kid's knew her, and many called her "Mom" although I found out later that she wasn't a biological mom to any of them.

When she stood up, the room fell silent. The man standing in the lobby watching through the glass reentered the sanctuary and took his seat. Every eye was set on Mom.

"I have something I want to say," She said. She explained that Beth had lived with them for several years. One morning, she had come in from her garden. Beth had been watching her from the window. When she went inside, Beth asked her, "Mom, are you high?" "No," she replied, "Why would you ask me that?" "Because you seem so happy." Said Beth. "Come with me, I want to show you something," she said. Mom took Beth's hand, and they walked out into the garden. They spent the whole morning working there. We tilled soil, pulled weeds, planted seeds, and cared for the sprouts just beginning to peek their heads up out into the spring sun. They took in the fresh air and the beauty of Mom's garden, just the two of them. They talked, and laughed—enjoyed their work. And when they were finished, Beth looked around at the beautiful garden, turned, looked at Mom and said, "I finally did something good." Mom cried, as she shared that now, every time she works in the garden she looks up into the window and wishes she could see Beth's beautiful blue eyes smiling back at her. "But it's too late for her," said Mom. Then she stood silently for a moment, taking the time to make eye contact with every single person in that room.

Mom didn't preach that day, didn't judge, didn't lecture. That crowd wouldn't have listened if she had. Yet everyone in that room got the point. Life is about choices, and sometimes the best ones are right in front of us. It takes work to plant a garden—there are weeds to pull, seeds to plant, and the soil needs nutrients. The day after the funeral I found out that Beth was shot on a Tuesday, and one week later she was scheduled to enter rehab. Mom wasn't able to save Beth with her garden, but as I looked around the sanctuary that day I could almost see Mom's seeds scattered about, making their way into the tiny cracks of hurting hearts. I could only pray that some would take root. After the service I asked if I could share (without real names) mom's wisdom with you, and thankfully I was given permission.

There are so many lessons to be learned in the garden. If there isn't some kind of garden outreach for teens, there should be. Charles Swindoll said, "Vision is spawned by faith, sustained by hope, sparked by imagination, and strengthened by enthusiasm." This is so true. Every great idea seems to begin this way. And it doesn't have to be rocket science. Here is a perfect (very simple) example. Over the years, as we've worked on the gardens and gutters of the seniors we serve in our community, we've seen some common needs, and one is for firewood. For many, this is their only heat source, so it made sense to us to start a separate division specifically for that purpose. With a little faith, hope, imagination, and enthusiasm, we now have an amazing firewood outreach. There is a group of people who procure firewood (talk people into letting them take logs and trees for free), as well as a firewood chopping team and a firewood delivery team. Volunteers cut rounds and split wood during spring and summer (and sometimes in the pouring rain of winter), so that we have a nice stockpile when the calls start coming in during the colder months. I would love to take this further though. Wouldn't it be great if someone started a mentoring program where the adults could teach kids to cut firewood (a wonderful skill to have), and while they were together they could talk about life, what it means to be a good friend, and making the right choices? And when they were finished, they could deliver the firewood to people in need and learn about community service. I hope someone reading this will take that ball and run with it. I believe that every young person, regardless of what they've been through, is filled with all the potential in the world, if only we will spend some time to look a little deeper. Helen Keller said, "Character is like the fire within the flint–latent until it is struck out of the stone. Observing the flint stone, who would think it contained the possibility of light? And so it is with the dark experiences of life. When they are met with courage, they let out sparks of spiritual light." Let's build a bonfire together.

One Little Thing

The first time we did a large outreach at church, everyone got together afterward to share their experiences. Approximately 1,500 people in the congregation served including pastors. This was the experience that one of our pastors shared.

> *My family was signed up to participate in Compassion Weekend. Our group was scheduled to plant trees and do yard work in the community. The weather had been terrible–rainy, wet and cold. I'm embarrassed to admit that I had been feeling irritated at the timing. "Why do we have to do this in the fall with all the rain? It's going to be wet and miserable. We should reschedule this outreach for the summer, when it isn't raining." But then I got a wake-up call. As the weekend drew near, the rain became even more severe, and a couple of days before, a huge flood occurred in our community destroying dozens of homes. Many of us (volunteers) were quickly moved from the projects we had been scheduled for, to flood relief. After shoveling mud for two days, hugging crying homeowners, and retrieving priceless photo albums, I realized that Compassion Weekend had been scheduled in the middle of the rains for a reason. We had mounted up an army of volunteers for one thing, but God intended to use them for another. When we are patient enough to wait on God and experience His plan rather than our own, amazing things can happen.*

Chapter 9

Ham and Cheese

I heard someone describe a skit they saw once in a local church. In the skit, a homeless man was sitting on a bench and a woman from the church walked up and sat down beside him. "This person needs Jesus," the church lady thought to herself. (Apparently, you could hear what she was thinking over the speaker system.) She was dressed in a nice suit and heels, brief case in one hand, lunch bag in the other. She began to quote the Bible, comment on how he might have ended up in this situation, and share the potential consequences of him not listening. The man just sat in silence. The woman's voice became a little more exuberant, a little more assertive. Out came the Bible, and the "example" of how to evangelize continued. The person relaying this story said she became so agitated watching this skit that she wanted to stand up on the pew and yell at the top of her lungs, "Are you blind? He's probably starving! Give him your stinkin' sandwich!"

When I heard this story, I remember thinking that I would have wanted to do the same thing. I think sometimes we can be so insensitive. A hungry man sits in front of us, and we think only of our own agenda with no regard for how he might be feeling. How could he possibly hear anything she had to say when his stomach was empty. I must admit that I have been scolded for this reason. I have been told that rather than "preaching with my hands" I should begin with my voice. But for me it's about relationship. I don't think you can begin a relationship by barreling over someone. I've heard too many horror stories of people who will never again set foot in a church because the last time they did, they felt attacked. As my Aunt Susan says, "There's something about singing that opens the soul." It's like that with serving and being served, too. I've had so many experiences where I simply loved and served without words, and I watched as hearts were softened. And oftentimes, those softened hearts begin to wonder why I'm there. One of the best parts of serving is when people ask me why I'm helping them. I'm always happy to answer that question. "What better way to show my love for God, than to love and help carry the burden of someone else He loves," I tell them. This response always leads to some great conversations. We need to care for one another. Here's a good illustration:

A holy man was having a conversation with God one day and said, "God, I would like to know what Heaven and Hell are like." God led the holy man to two doors. He opened one of the doors, and the holy man looked in. In the middle of the room was a large round table. In the middle of the table was a large pot of stew, which smelled delicious and made the holy man's mouth water. The people sitting around the table were thin and sickly. They appeared to be famished. They were holding two spoons with very long handles that were strapped to their arms, and each found it possible to reach into the pot of stew and take a spoonful. But because the handle was longer than their arms, they could not get the spoons back into their mouths. The holy man shuddered at the sight of their misery and suffering. God said, "You have seen Hell." They went to the next room and opened the door. It was exactly the same as the first one. There was a large round table with the large pot of stew, which made the holy man's mouth water. The people were equipped with the same long-handled spoons, but here the people were well nourished and plump laughing and talking. The holy man said, "I don't understand." "It is simple" said God. "It requires but one skill. You see, they have learned to feed each other, while the greedy think only of themselves." (Author Unknown)

I was listening to a local radio station as people were calling in to share compassion stories. One of the listeners called with an amazing story. I was so intrigued by this that I did some research to find out what happened. The man in this story was anything but greedy. He was willing, not only to give an incredible gift to someone—a gift that would save a person's life, but he wanted the gift to be given to a complete stranger. He decided that he wanted to donate a kidney to anyone who was a match and needed it. Once he decided he wanted to do this, he talked to his wife, and began researching the process. He found The Living Donor Program at New York Presbyterian Hospital, which works with people who want to donate a kidney to a loved one, but aren't a match. Apparently, the average waiting time for a kidney in the United States is 3-5 years. Unfortunately for some, that wait can be fatal. Once the man decided to donate his kidney, he unknowingly started a chain of kidney swapping that resulted in saving four lives-eight surgeries in one day.

As it turns out, his kidney was a match for a woman who had been told she could be waiting five years for a transplant. Her husband wasn't a match for her, but he was willing to donate a kidney in return. The husband's kidney turned out to be a match for another woman. That woman's father (whose kidney was not a match for his daughter) then donated his kidney, which was a match for another man. This man's sister wasn't a match for her brother, but she too was willing to "pay it forward" and give her kidney to another person in need. As it turned out, she was a match for a man she has now nicknamed "lucky"- kidney recipient number four that day. Talk about a ripple affect! That was unquestionably a gift that kept on giving.

None of those people knew each other, yet every soul is tailored from the same fabric: "Neighbors" by divine proximity. With a little faith and a lot of courage, as each person stepped outside the land of me, a perfect circle of compassion was formed. Gifts given–one to another.

When we think of gifts, we sometimes think of tangible items. We've all given and received gifts throughout our lives, some more meaningful than others. But, oftentimes, it's the intangible gifts that hold the greatest value. I got into a conversation recently with some friends about whether we had ever received a sacrificial gift that humbled us–tangible or intangible. I thought of the little girl at the ranch that gave her only soccer ball to my son Coleton. I thought of hats and scarves knitted for me by the blind women my grandmother visited, and wonderful things from other countries given to me by Habitat families wanting to say "thank you" or share a bit of their culture with me. In every instance I felt moved by the generosity of those with so little willing to give so much. One of the stories shared was about an intangible gift given. A friend of mine has two girls who take piano lessons once a week. They love to go because the piano teacher is fun and creative and lets them choose songs that are current and relevant to them. He jokes with them about all his tattoos and piercings, telling them to "be careful about this stuff–people will judge you based on your appearance." But then he will pray with them if they want, and the girls know he loves them. Times had been tight for this family, and my friend had come to the realization that they could no longer afford piano lessons. This made her incredibly sad because the girls loved it so much, and she felt bad for the teacher who was a small business owner and counted on those lessons for his income. She had been gathering up the courage for a couple of weeks to tell the teacher and the girls that the lessons would have to stop until they could get back on their feet financially. Lesson day finally arrived and she cried, choking out the bad news. "Don't worry," the teacher said. "You just keep coming every week, just like always–no charge. If you have a little money now and then, pay what you can, and if you have none, just bring the girls anyway. You don't owe me anything." My friend cried as she told us this story of an incredibly generous gift given during a difficult time.

This makes me think of all the people in this world who are retired or momentarily unemployed. The pool of talents must be immeasurable. Imagine what would happen if they took a little bit of their time each week, or each month to help a non-profit or someone in need. They might be surprised–the connections made and experience gained could potentially result in a brand new career. It's so easy to get caught up in our own version of what we believe our destiny to be that we become unable to veer off that predetermined path. Sometimes, we just need to open our eyes and see where God might be leading us. Many people find that when they do this, the destination (and the journey) ends up being so much better than anything they ever could have planned. You might be saying to yourself "But I don't have any gifts or talents that could be used to help someone". Everyone has gifts and talents. They were given to you by God for a purpose. I've spoken to people who think that life is random, a big mistake-that an individual's birth is really meaningless in the big scheme of things-we are born, we live, we die. They couldn't be more wrong. The Bible says, "For you created my inmost being; you knit me together in my mother's womb. Praise you because I am fearfully and wonderfully made; your works are wonderful, I know that full well. My frame was not hidden from you when I was made in the secret place. When I was woven together in the depths of the earth, your eyes saw my unformed body. All the days ordained for me were written in your book before one of them came to be." Psalms 139:13-16. You are wonderfully made, and you were created with a purpose in mind. We should never compare ourselves with others, because we're all so unique. Some of us are good with children, some with cooking or hospitality, some may have artistic abilities. Maybe you can build things, or you are a compassionate person who has the gift of being able to sit quietly with someone who needs to talk, or perhaps you are an excellent teacher. You were born for a reason. God knows each of us intimately. A great illustration of this was when Jesus used the metaphor of the shepherd and his sheep. He said that the shepherd "called" each sheep by name. Don't think for one minute that your life is random. God knows you by name.

I sometimes wonder what God thinks when we don't use our gifts and talents. Have you ever carefully chosen a gift for someone you loved, but when you gave it to them, you could tell by their response that they really didn't like it? It can hurt your feelings. I think God must feel the same way when we don't appreciate, or use the gifts He's given us.

We are supposed to use our gifts and talents to work together in unity. We need everyone to be able to complete the tasks God has in mind for us. We are one body with many (important) parts. "As it is, there are many parts, but one body. The eye cannot say to the hand, "I don't need you!" And the head cannot say to the feet, "I don't need you!" On the contrary, those parts of the body that seem to be weaker are indispensable, and the parts that we think are less honorable we treat with special honor. And the parts that are unpresentable are treated with special modesty, while our presentable parts need no special treatment. But God has combined the members of the body and has given greater honor to the parts that lacked it, so that there should be no division in the body, but that its parts should have equal concern for each other. If one part suffers, every part suffers with it; if one part is honored, every part rejoices with it." 1 Corinthians 12:20-26. You are a critical part of the body.

I urge you to ask God to help you to find your specific gifts or talents, and how you should be using them. If you are not sure what your gifts and talents are, there are ways of finding out. Three different resources that can help you get started are; SHAPE Curriculum, Online Gifts Tests, and a book called, "Discover Your God-Given Talents and Inspire your Community" by Albert L. Winseman, Donald O. Clifton, and Curt Liesvield. Knowing what you were created for will help direct your path.

Kelly's path was a rocky one. She had a lot to teach me about trusting God. Her story is incredible. The obstacles she overcame seemed insurmountable to me, yet she didn't just prevail, she prevailed with grace and dignity.

The distance in miles between Kelly and the children that had been taken from her was two thousand, one hundred sixteen. Like so many women, Kelly had been living within the horrors of domestic violence. She had finally summoned up the courage to divorce her husband, only to have him kidnap her children during an unsupervised visit and move them from Texas to Washington. And this wasn't the first time. Several times during this process, even though the courts had granted her custody, he had taken the kids, and she had to find them and bring them home. Having walked away from the marriage with almost nothing, she sold what little she had and got on a plane to try and bring her children home again. No friends, no family, no car, and very little money. Not long before I met Kelly, she had been living in a tent, struggling with the courts to try and get her children back from a man she feared. And through it all Kelly says she prayed, "Humble me, Lord". She wanted God to soften her heart from pride, anger, and feelings of revenge for what had been done to her. I can almost guarantee I would not have had that much grace.

I asked how she did it, and she told me that with the help of many kindnesses from individuals along the way and a lot of prayer, she "put one foot in front of the other each day". She started cleaning houses and saved enough money to rent a small duplex and buy an old car. Eventually, she was able to get her children back. She met a woman named Cory who hangs out at the Skate Park at night helping teens and homeless people any way she can. One night, Cory gave her gas money so she'd have a way to get to work the next day. At the time, Kelly was living in a completely empty duplex–no silverware, beds, couch, nothing. Cory stopped by a garage sale one day and talked the sellers into giving all the furniture and kitchen items they had for sale to Kelly for free. Kelly started attending our church, and during the difficult times she would call for help. When her car broke down, a volunteer named Jeff replaced the radiator for free. When she needed food, she stopped by our little food pantry, and during the time her car was being repaired, volunteers delivered the food to her house. When she needed a little extra money to keep the lights turned on one month, the church, along with Love inc., was able to help. Kelly's eyes welled with tears as she told me how much the Giving Tree meant to her and her children at Christmas time.

I now consider Kelly a friend. We volunteer every month together with an organization called Angel Food Ministries. When I asked Kelly if I could tell her story, she said yes if I used a different name (for the sake of her children). I asked where she got the courage to keep going. She asked me to tell you that that we should never doubt God, because He will always provide. She wanted you to know how much each act of kindness, no matter how small, meant to her. And she wanted me to tell you that when you do something kind for another person, it helps that person see that "God hasn't forgotten about them. It gives them hope and the courage to go on." So you see that it doesn't take a lot to change a life–just a little compassion. And, in Kelly's case, she has gone on to help others through service projects and volunteer work. The drop becomes a ripple.

An amazing person I met with LFC (our senior outreach) was Henry. Henry is a character. Slow southern drawl. Rough around the edges. Drives an old, beat up van. I met him when the alternator on his vehicle had gone out. Someone had told him to give me a call, and he did. At the time, I didn't think much of it. Jeff, (our car repair volunteer), said he would fix it for free if Henry could get it up to Jeff's place. Since Henry didn't have anyone to help pull his car to Jeff's place, I found a towing company that would tow it for a reduced rate, which we ended up paying for out of our LFC account. Several days later, Henry had picked up his van in good working order. Many months went by, and I didn't think about Henry after that, until he pulled up early one morning in front of our offices looking for me. His van was there, and at first I thought there might be something else that needed fixing. Henry came to give me a hug. He just wanted to say thank you. We chatted for a few minutes, and then, as he walked toward his van, he nonchalantly told me that before the person had told him to call me about his van, he had planned his suicide. He was done trying. Life had gotten too hard, and it seemed like nobody really cared. He had made a plan to kill himself by jumping off the viaduct onto the freeway.

I stood there staring at him in disbelief. I hit rewind on my brain, and the memories of the day he called came flooding back to me. He had told me about his van, and I was pretty sure Jeff would fix it. But we had never towed anyone before. We don't do this because we get so many calls for car repairs, and simply don't have the funds for towing. I had asked him if he had an old chain or rope, that someone could use to tow him up there, and he didn't. He didn't seem to have anyone. What in the world made me start calling towing companies? It wasn't in the budget. I had told Henry I would call him back in fifteen minutes with an answer. Again, what was I thinking? I had never done that either. I always give myself a couple hours. And what was I thinking trying to find a towing company to drive out to the boonies where Henry lived at what was going to have to be a very deep discount, and to find that towing company in fifteen minutes? And then having them actually say yes, and within 15 minutes calling Henry back, and within an hour after that, having the tow truck driver pull up to his house. The hair was standing up on the back of my neck. At the time, for some reason, none of this stood out to me as even remotely unusual. I won't take credit for any of it because, clearly, the chain of events had been God-driven. And when I asked Henry to tell me more, a story unfolded that blew my mind.

In Henry's life, he'd lost a wife and child, gotten involved with drugs, and been in prison. But he told me his life has changed now. He said that if he can go through all that and still have hope, and keep going, anyone can. The person who told him to call me about the van invited him to start attending this group called Celebrate Recovery. It seems to have changed his life. He now goes a couple hours early to share his story and offer support to other people who might be struggling. It seemed like an echo when he told me (as Kelly had) that when he looks back now, he can see that God always provided for him. He told me that each time he got stuck along the way and felt hopeless (even the final time when he was about to give up), someone stopped what they were doing and offered just what he needed at that moment–a bite to eat, a kind word, a car repair. And as we were saying goodbye he told me a story. Apparently, the other day, he was driving down the freeway and saw a couple's car had broken down. He pulled his van over and went back to ask them what was wrong. They were embarrassed to tell him that they had run out of gas. "I have some gas in the back of my van," said Henry, and he went back to get it. "We can't take your gas," they said. "At least let us give you money for it." Henry emptied his gas can into their car and replied; "You don't owe me anything. God must have given me that gas so I could give it to you. I'm sure He'll give me more." He wished them well, and said goodbye. No one could ever convince me that that couple wasn't changed forever that day because a simple act of kindness by an unlikely benefactor.

Henry isn't perfect, he still struggles and has difficulties, but he taught me that serving is about the connection between faith and deeds. Not deeds for the purpose of getting some kind of reward in return, but deeds simply because it's the right thing to do. James 2:14 -17 says: "What good is it, my brothers, if a man claims to have faith but has no deeds? Can such faith save him? Suppose a brother or sister is without clothes and daily food. If one of you says to him, 'Go, I wish you well; keep warm and well fed,' but does nothing about his physical needs, what good is it? In the same way, faith by itself, if it is not accompanied by action, is dead."

Years ago, if a woman committed murder in a domestic violence situation, the abuse couldn't be brought up during the trial unless she could prove that her life was in danger at the moment she committed the murder. The abuse was considered irrelevant to the case. The subject of domestic violence was taboo, and what went on between husband and wife was between them–it was considered personal. This was the case for Barbara.

Almost thirty years ago, Barbara was a victim of domestic violence. She had endured many years of abuse including a night where her husband beat her so badly at the tavern they owned in front of all the patrons that as she lay on the floor, he continued kicking her in the head while the people at the bar watched. Those years also included the time he beat her until she lost consciousness, drove out to the country, and threw her in a ditch. One night it all ended. Barbara snapped and killed him. And the world suddenly grew silent. At first, for her it was like walking around in a coma. She was in prison, separated from her children. In some ways, the world was peaceful–not waiting for the next explosion, but in other ways it was horrific, as she watched her family ripped from her, wondering if she'd ever see them again. Also, to live with taking another person's life, regardless of the situation, "haunts a person forever." As the trial went on, it became clear that she would be sent to prison for essentially a lifetime.

She got used to it after a while–the routine of it. But it was hard to hold on to any kind of hope, knowing that a life in prison without her family was really "it" for her. At first, her children were able to come and see her, but as the years went on the visits became fewer and farther between. After a while she wondered, "What's the point, anyway?" It only created a burden for them to visit her there. After close to twenty years in prison, she said she reached the point one evening where she really believed it might be easier for her children if she were dead. She leaned against the bed in the corner of her cell and peeked out the small window there. She told God, "I can't do this anymore–I'm sorry, but I just can't go on." She said the sun was beginning to set, and the sky was filled with purple and gold.

All of a sudden, a shaft of light hit the wire on the fence, and traveled down the entire length, which made the wire disappear. And then as the light stretched and glowed across the wires and buildings, reflecting and illuminating everything, the entire prison seemed to disappear. All she could see were the mountains, trees and miles of fields, as if she were standing outside the prison–free. "There will be freedom," she heard God

105

say, in the depths of her soul. And she knew then that freedom would come, and she would know a life again outside those prison walls.

Not long after that, Barbara was connected with my Aunt Susan who volunteers for an organization called WICS that helps people who have lived in prison for many years transition into the "outside" world. They begin before the person gets out of prison, visiting them and getting to know them. They start teaching them skills, like how to fill out a job application, how to set up a bank account, and how to balance a checkbook. These seem like such simple things to many, but if you've lived within the structure of prison life for long enough, it's very difficult to remember (or learn) how to do these things.

Aunt Susan and Barbara developed a friendship, and finally one day those prison gates opened and she walked out. Barbara said that before prison she felt like a caterpillar, crawling around on the ground, just trying desperately to stay out of the way, hoping not to get stepped on. The prison for her was a cocoon. She was living in the dark, completely wrapped in fear, worry, and stress. But the day those doors opened and she walked out into the light, she was a butterfly—happy now and finally free. "Sometimes God waits until the last minute," Barbara said. "Sometimes it just seems like too much. But God is with you, refining you, walking with you every step. And just when you feel you can't take one more step, he steps ahead of you, opens the door and out you fly."

The subtitle of this book is "The Little Things Do Matter." This was precisely the case with Barbara. She credits my Aunt (and her church) with her success in the "real" world. Aunt Susan helped her with rent and utilities her first three months. She gave her clothes and shoes to wear, and bought her bus tickets. She taught her how to get a social security card and took her to the DMV—which can be a nightmare even if you haven't been in prison—and got her an ID card. And what she couldn't tell her she wrote down in a notebook. The notebook contained detailed instructions on how to do such things as ride the bus, get food stamps, and do a food budget. During the times they couldn't be together, Barbara could use the notebook to help her navigate through a new (and scary) life. "The difference," said Barbara, "is this."

She told me that when she first got out, she met with a couple who wanted to try and help her get started. (This was before Aunt Susan's notebook.) The meeting ended and Barbara told them she didn't have any food. She asked if they could tell her where to go to get food stamps. "It's in the phone book," said the wife. Barbara wondered how in the world she would find that information in the phone book. (By the way, it's not listed under food stamps. You have to know to look for DSHS.) Then Barbara asked how she would get to the food stamps office, and the husband said, "You will need to learn to take the bus." They weren't anywhere near a bus line at the time, and she didn't have a listing of the buses and their routes. "This is the difference between going through the motions and truly wanting to help someone," said Barbara. "Your heart is either in it or it isn't." Aunt Susan's heart was in it from the beginning.

Barbara now lives on a total of $640 per month, and she's happy. She says that after what she has experienced, you learn that superficial things don't matter. As long as your basic human needs are met, what matters are the people in your lives and your relationships. Barbara is in her seventies now and volunteers each summer at a kid's camp which hosts foster kids ages 7 – 11, who have been severely emotionally and physically abused. It gives them the opportunity to "just be a kid" as they fish, swim, and play ball. "They even get to cook the trout they catch!" They are taught that they have a father (God) who loves them unconditionally, is with them every moment, and would never hurt them. The leaders plan a birthday party for each kid while they are there, including a cake and presents. "Many of them have never had a birthday party before, so this experience is amazing," says Barbara.

Additionally, Barbara is in the process of starting her own prison ministry. She learned while she was in prison that if you don't have family, friends, or a church or other support group to come visit you, you begin to lose hope. And without a positive support system, it is almost impossible for you to succeed when you finally get out. This is part of the reason why so many long-term inmates end up committing crimes and going right back into prison as soon as they get out. They can't do it on their own. Developing these relationships helps you learn to respect yourself and others. Barbara says, "People can still grow and develop in prison. The body may be behind bars, but the mind is always free, and God is always with you." She wants to set up a non-profit that provides transportation to family members of inmates, helping them travel to the prison and visit. She also wants to create an organization that will manage visitation and support prisoners who don't have any family to visit them, so every person in prison has someone who cares about them. "This can make all the difference."

Barbara also speaks at colleges about domestic violence and encourages young women to "get out before it's too late and something terrible happens." And although she knows God has forgiven her, she shares what it's like to have to live with what she did for the rest of her life. Today when people ask Barbara what they can do to help, she says, "Be a friend to someone." That friendship can be a safe harbor in the midst of a storm.

Five Little Things

1. Thank You Treats
The men and women who protect and serve, put their lives on the line every day for us, and many times there's no "thank you" for their hard work. Bake a bunch of treats and drop them off at your local fire or police station with a thank you note.

2. Book'em, Dano
In a struggling economy, many people have to turn off their internet and cable, and put a stop to book purchases and movie rentals. At the library, they can use the internet, and check out books and movies for free. Go through all your old books and movies and donate some to your local public library.

3. Get Fired Up!
You might be surprised at how many low-income people heat their homes with wood. Find someone that uses wood as their primary heat source in the winter and deliver a load of split firewood to them.

4. Share a Meal
There's nothing better than a home cooked meal—especially when you don't have to cook it! These days, many people work more than one job, or for other reasons, they simply aren't able to cook. Find a busy working mom, single guy, or senior in your neighborhood and take a home made hot dinner to them one night.

5. Color Someone's World
My daughter Jess came home the other day after she had been at the grocery store with my friend Anne. Apparently Anne made quite an impression when she bought a bouquet of flowers and upon checkout, gave them to the grocery clerk and asked her to give them as a gift to the next person who seemed to be having a bad day. Brighten someone's day the next time you are at the grocery store.

Ham and Cheese

Chapter 10

———— ❀ ————

And They're Off!

Being a veterinarian, I had been called to examine a ten-year-old Irish Wolfhound named Belker. The dog's owners, Ron, his wife Lisa, and their little boy Shane, were all very attached to Belker, and they were hoping for a miracle.

I examined Belker and found he was dying of cancer. I told the family we couldn't do anything for Belker, and offered to perform the euthanasia procedure for the old dog in their home. As we made arrangements, Ron and Lisa told me they thought it would be good for six-year old Shane to observe the procedure. They felt as though Shane might learn something from the experience. The next day, I felt the familiar catch in my throat as Belker's family surrounded him. Shane seemed so calm, petting the old dog for the last time, that I wondered if he understood what was going on. Within a few minutes, Belker slipped peacefully away.

The little boy seemed to accept Belker's transition without any difficulty or confusion. We sat together for a while after Beleker's death, wondering aloud about the sad fact that animal lives are shorter than human lives. Shane who had been listening quietly, piped up. "I know why." Startled, we all turned to him. What came out of his mouth next stunned me. I'd never heard a more comforting explanation. He said, "People are born so that they can learn how to live a good life–like loving everybody all the time and being nice right?" The six year old continued, "Well dogs already know how to do that, so they don't have to stay as long." (author unknown)

Hopefully it won't take us a lifetime to learn to "love everybody all the time and be nice." I pray you'll take the lessons contained in this book and use them to make your life, and someone else's–or lots of someone else's–a little better. Be a daisy picker. When you come to the end of your days, are you really going to remember (or care) what the "crowd" thought, or are you going to care about the legacy of love and friendship you left behind? Remember to look up, open your eyes and notice those around you – then do something about it. The little things do matter–even those five-minute interactions can impact another person's life. I hope you will begin to live your life with intention – as if you "mean it", so people (like the greeter at church) can look into your eyes and see that you are fully present in that moment. When we look at people, we need to see what's behind their eyes – there's a soul in there. Mathew 25: 35 – 40 says; "For I was hungry, and you fed me, I was thirsty, and you gave me a drink. I was a stranger, and you invited me into your home. I was naked, and you gave me clothing. I was sick, and you cared for me. I was in prison, and you visited me. Then these righteous ones will reply, 'Lord, when did we ever see you hungry and feed you? Or thirsty and give you something to drink? Or a stranger and show you hospitality? Or naked and give you clothing? When did we ever see you sick or in prison and visit you? And the King will say, 'I tell you the truth, when you did it to one of the least of these my brothers and sisters, you were doing it to me!' The scruffy guy holding the sign? God in skin. You may never know the outcome of your actions toward that "scruffy" guy. Maybe the outcome is the kindness itself providing the gift of hope, or peace. So stop what you are doing, bend down, and talk to the lady (who is talking to herself) in the wheelchair. God in skin. I trust you'll begin to see people with a new set of eyes–eyes that see that agape love is God-driven, and is meant to be selfless and unconditional. We tend to use our own experiences as a gauge, but we really have no idea where someone else might be coming from. You may need to adjust your agenda. If you tell a cold, hungry homeless man that God loves him, do you think he'll listen? What if you feed him, give him a blanket, or find him a safe place to lay his head at night? Will he listen then? Don't tell him, show him. Then later, when his basic human needs are met, he may hear you. And if he doesn't hear you, love him anyway.

I'm praying every day that you'll play that beautiful note of yours and watch it resonate out into the world in perfect harmony. Just think of the changed lives in Elly's life when Maryanne played that one little note then sat in awe as it rippled all the way to Africa and back. No matter who you are, you can change the world. Many times the lives you touch (those

112

in need), become the needed, as they too step out and begin to change the world. If we drop those barriers (the lines that separate "us" from "them"), we can *be* the church in the world–the kind of church I think Jesus loves–the kind with no walls to lock people out. Do you remember the Starfish Parable? "I made a difference to that one." One is something. Sometimes one is everything.

We shouldn't charge interest for our time. That sacrifice (time, energy, even money) is just that–a sacrifice–one made for the One who made us. I think of Mrs. Mauer taking me to those events–instead of going with Ronnie and her husband or one of her own girls. And I think of all the people I can't even begin to list, like the woman from our church who took my brother and I in for a week when we both had the chicken pox and my dad was working. Sacrifice. Love. Aren't they really the same thing? Even if you don't feel worthy of the sacrifice, remember that sometimes, because of those reasons, you are the very person who should be making the sacrifice. It's tough to offer up your true self, but your history is part of your destiny. If someone is struggling with addiction, are they going to listen to someone who's never had an addiction problem? Probably not.

I think of Tina, and those little acts of kindness–a sandwich, a shed, a prayer–that gave her a glimpse of God and helped restore her dignity. She discovered that her hope had been misplaced, and she learned to turn to God when the things of this world let her down. Those who served her watched her health and happiness restored. And sometimes the restoration of health happens in the life of the volunteer as well. I'm asking you to try (even if you feel unable, unworthy, sick, or sad) taking the focus off your own situation and directing that attention to someone else in need. As you help them restore their health or dignity, you might just recapture a bit of your own. As the statistics earlier in this book show, one of the reasons volunteering is good for your health is the increase in social networking. We were made to be in community with one another. I highly recommend you try to find another person, or group of people to consistently serve alongside, study with, learn with, and grow together. I don't think I could function without my Bible study group or my closest girlfriends. In both cases, we've been together for years, and lived through many of the struggles of life that come with time. We've supported each other through late nights with colicky babies and teen-ager drama, death, illness, and divorce. We've laughed and cried together, shared a good healthy debate, and stood beside one another when a little extra dose of courage was in order. If you don't know where to start, find a good community church. If they don't have groups, keep looking until you find one that does.

Remember that God *is* love. And since we are created in His image, we are called to *be* love. Life is not a game of craps. It may seem that way sometimes, but it isn't. You have a purpose, and the clock is ticking. Don't gamble with the time you have; it may end tomorrow. If you haven't found your purpose, just pray, step out in faith, and do what you know to be right. God will equip you with the tools you'll need and continue to guide you forward. And if you hear, "What are you going to do now Jonah?" have a good chuckle and know that God isn't finished with you yet.

The world moves so quickly these days, and I worry about the impact the felt need for immediacy has on our children. We want more, so we work harder to get more, but then there's more to want. We need to teach our children the concept of plentitude–the idea that there is a difference between needs and wants, and in many cases, what children have is plenty. We can model this by helping them to see the world through someone else's eyes as we give them a chance to love and serve a person who might have things a little tougher than they do. This experience can be life-changing. The children of this world are watching everything we do. Good or bad, they are gleaning what they can from us. We should be teaching them what it means to be kind, as they witness compassion in the lives of the adults to which they are exposed. Remember that children will oftentimes pay more attention to what we do than what we say. Sometimes we need to "preach with our hands," not just with our words. I hope you'll plant a seed in the life of a child and watch it grow.

Remember that singular acts of kindness can result in a multitude of blessings. I'm reminded of Darren (from Cambodia) and the thousands of lives he now impacts for the better because of a brave man with a shovel, a missionary, and a group of Habitat volunteers–all neighbors by divine proximity. We live in different countries, we have different cultures and religions, and we belong to different socio-economic groups, yet we are still all neighbors in God's eyes. We need to remember to love our "neighbor" as ourselves, regardless of that which may seem to divide us. We could all learn some lessons from Darren in this area. We need to be grateful. Rather than complaining about what we don't have, we should use what we do to the fullest.

Today is the day. No "buts." That one little thing you do–treating someone to a coffee, giving a hug, acknowledging someone else's pain–

might be the very thing that reminds that person that God has not forgotten them. And your gifts, whether tangible or intangible, could lead you in a whole new direction. Don't allow yourself to get stuck. Community, encouragement, and compassion–remember the goose. We need to be unified, and sometimes we need to do the practical to get to the spiritual. You can be confident that God will provide for those practical needs. It may not always look the way you thought it might, but pray, then watch as the needs are met–one way or the other–and it won't be a "coincidence."

As I write these final words, I'm awestruck by God's timing. I finished this book in June, took some time off, and then began working with my editor in late Fall. In January, we were editing the last chapter, and because of some changes in the resources, he asked me to add an additional story and a synopsis of the lessons contained in the book. I spent several days stymied for the right story. I felt it needed to be a story that demonstrated the importance of stepping outside ourselves and interacting with the world around us. The story needed to show a life lived with compassion and love. After racking my brain for the better part of a week, I asked my husband if he had any ideas, and without skipping a beat he said, "Well, Howard, of course." Howard. The perfect example.

Last June, my daughter Jessie and I spent the day with two of our LFC volunteers, clearing a piece of property for an eighty-year old woman who needed some help. One of the volunteers was a guy in his fifties, named Howard. We spent the day having fun, working hard, and Howard had the best time teasing my teenaged daughter the whole day in that sweet, gentle way of his. He and another volunteer named Chris asked if they could build a fire with all of the debris, and rather than taking more stuff to the landfill, I said, "Sure, let's do it!" Chris and Howard's faces lit up like two ten-year-old boys who'd just been given a package of firecrackers. That was quite the bonfire they built that day. It was always like that with Howard. There seemed to be a child-like quality to him. He lived in the moment and took experiences and people in, as if they were all new somehow. He has always been one of my most faithful LFC volunteers. Anytime I called him, he said yes–for a car repair, yard work, ditch digging– anything. He was one of those people who preached with his hands, his back, and his heart. But Howard also preached with his voice–not at a pulpit, but in a gentle, personal way. He wanted everyone to know the message of Christ. And our ministry wasn't the only one Howard served under. He was also an usher and greeter at the church. He was one of those wonderful smiling faces greeting those that enter the church each Sunday morning. Howard was perfect for this job because he truly had no preconceived notions about people. He didn't judge, he just smiled that big, charming smile of his and made you feel welcome.

After several years of serving with LFC, in addition to the lessons Howard taught me, I got to find out all kinds of personal things about him. Apparently, he rode his bike in the Seattle-to-Portland race for the first time not long ago. His now grown boys loved to tease him about his bright yellow "manly" spandex outfit. I got to see his amazing bow hunting equipment, and this cool jeep he lovingly restored over some twenty years. Howard made the most of every day and took the time to nurture relationships with those he loved. I saw pictures of his three boys, embraced by their dad, and found out that he adopted them as pre-teens and teens when he married their mother. And when you saw him with his beautiful bride Betty, you knew it was truly a marriage made in heaven.

Earlier in the book, I wrote about God's providential timing. He never ceases to amaze me, and here's one last example. As I mentioned, I finished this book in June of 2009. In June, Howard, Chris, Jessie, and I were clearing land at the senior's house. In August Howard went into the doctor for some discomfort in his arm, and shortly after, he was diagnosed with ALS (Lou Gehrig's Disease). By October Howard could no longer walk and was bound to a wheel chair. Those he served alongside in LFC were building a handicap ramp to his house. By December, he'd lost the use of most of his body, and the ushers he served with were at his house stringing Christmas lights outside his window so that he might enjoy the magic of one last glorious Christmas. And on December 30th, 2009, Howard Wellington unzipped that ALS-racked body and headed home. I find it interesting that I wasn't asked to add one last story until the story I needed was complete. God's providential timing. Not long after his death, we had Howard's memorial. I stood in the back, scanning a packed house. Tears ran down my cheeks as I listened to those he loved recount a life well-lived. And it occurred to me, as I stood there taking it all in, how tenuous our lives are here in this place we temporarily call home.

I hope this little book has encouraged you to consider leaving "the land of me." There's a world of possibility out there; we just need to open the door and take that first step—one that could change another person's life. Remember that God isn't sitting in a building somewhere waiting for the people to come. Don't misunderstand me; I need my church. It's there that

I learn, grow, and form relationships. But God isn't waiting there in that building for me. He is in me, and He's in you. And if that doesn't blow your mind, it should. As Dale Tacket reminds us, "The Creator of the Universe dwells within you." We should feel privileged to be His hands and feet. C.S. Lewis said, "You don't have a soul; You are a soul. You have a body." One day, like Howard, we'll unzip this body and go home. But for now, I'm asking you to join me on a journey... leaving the land of me.

And They're Off!

Let's Get Started!

The following pages contain a list of the non-profit organizations I mention in the book. These are just a few of the thousands of serving opportunities available today. I've included this list to make it a little bit easier to get started, but if you don't see anything that interests you here, just visit my website at www.leavingthelandofme.com to get more serving ideas, read more stories, and maybe share a story of your own!

And They're Off!

Organization	Who They Serve	Mission	Contact Information
Habitat for Humanity	Families	To turn the dream of home ownership into reality for those in poverty or who are homeless …to eliminate poverty & homelessness	www.habitat.org Operational Headquarters Habitat for Humanity International 121 Habitat Street Americus, GA 31709-3498 USA 1-800-422-4828
Love, Inc. (Love In the Name of Christ)	Families Adults Youth Seniors Churches	Brings Christian churches together to help the poor by meeting needs such as food, clothing, & relational ministries such as life skills training & transitional housing. Helps churches form networks to cover the community needs and provided coordination for more comprehensive community coverage. Training for young people to educate them about poverty and equip them to take action.	www.loveinc.org 800-777-5277
The Dream Center	Inner-cities: Adults Families Youth Seniors	Meets tangible & spiritual needs by providing food, clothing, shelter, life rehabilitation, education, job training & Biblical training. Short-term missions and internships available.	www.dreamcenter.org 213-273-7000 Los Angeles
Meals on Wheels,	Seniors	Provides meals to Seniors who would not otherwise eat properly for a more healthy and enjoyable life, as well as provide human contact and friendship	http://www.mealcall.org/meals-on-wheels
BRAVE Foundation	People of Guatem-ala	Group of Local Puyallup Firefighters started organization to improve the fire and life saving efforts in Guatemala. Short and long term missions available.	www.bravefoundation.org 253-970-4330 Puyallup Headquarters
KiteGang	Children	By lifting the spirits of children who have very little through the joy & curiosity of kites	http://www.kitegang.org/ 612-600-5791 612-251-1606 Minneapolis, MN
Lions4Kids	Youth	To provide needy children clothes, personal care items, school supplies & other resources so they are nicely attired, clean, groomed & outfitted for learning to boost self-image and success in school	http://lions4kids.com/aboutus.aspx 253-447-3844 Bonney Lake, WA
Lions Club	Families Men Women Youth	Groups interested in improving their communities & international communities	http://www.lionsclubs.org 630-571-5466 Headquarters, Oakbrook, IL
Freezing Nights	Homeless	Churches open their doors when wind chill is 35 degrees for homeless – October through March	http://www.pnconline.org/281696.ihtml 253-309-8618

121

Organization	Who They Serve	Mission	Contact Information
		Sponsor: Puyallup Church of the Nazarene & other local churches	Other similar programs nationally
Oral Hull Foundation for the Blind	The Blind	Historic 23-acre park and camp for the visually impaired. Picnic shelter, indoor swimming pool, rec room, hot tub, jogging track, fire pit and childrens' playground. Gardens emphasize use of all five senses.	www.oralhull.org 43233 SE Oral Hull Road, Sandy, Oregon, United States 503-668-6195
Little Bit Special Riders	Children and Adults	improving the bodies, minds and spirits of children and adults with disabilities through equine-assisted therapy and to be an inspiration and educational resource to the therapeutic riding profession, both regionally and nationally.	www.littlebit.org 19802 N.E. 148th St. Woodinville, WA 98077 425-882-1554
Safe Streets	Neighbors	Empowering individuals, families, youth, neighbors, and organizations to create safe neighborhoods.	www.safest.org 1501 Pacific Avenue, Suite 305 Tacoma, WA 98402 253-594-7838 Available Nationally
Alcoholics Anonymous	People struggling with Alcohol Addiction	Alcoholics Anonymous is a fellowship of men and women who share their experience, strength and hope with each other that they may solve their common problem and help others to recover from Alcoholism.	www.aa.org P.O. Box 459 New York, NY 10163 212-870-3400
World Vision Chicken//Goat Purchase	Families struggling in third world countries	World Vision is a Christian relief, development and advocacy organization dedicated to working with children, families and communities to overcome poverty and injustice.	www.worldvision.org P.O. Box 9716 Federal Way, WA 98063 (888)511-6443
Rancho Sordo Mudo	Deaf children in Mexico	Rancho Sordo Mudo is a free Christian home and school for deaf Mexican children.	luke@ranchosordomudo.org FROM US: 011-52-646-155-2201 FROM WITHIN MEXICO: 01-646-155-2201 P.O. Box 7441 Chula Vista, CA 91912
Hoops of Hope	AIDS Orphans	Hoops of Hope is the biggest basketball shoot-a-thon in the world, much like a walk-a-thon, but more fun! Every dollar raised will go directly to the project you select to help these children	www.hoopsofhope.org PO Box 22227 Mesa, AZ 85277 (480) 231-4501
Celebrate Recovery	Those struggling with addictive behaviors	To fellowship and celebrate God´s healing power in our lives through the "8 Recovery Principles."	www.celebraterecovery.com (949) 609-8305.
WICS	Low	Women in Community Service's	www.wics.org

Organization	Who They Serve	Mission	Contact Information
	income, disadvant aged women and youth.	mission is to reduce the number of women and youth living in poverty by promoting self-reliance and economic independence.	1900 N Beauregard St Suite 103 Alexandria, VA 22311
Big Brothers Big Sisters	Children 5 – 18	Big Brothers Big Sisters of America establishes and supervises mentoring relationships between adults and children ages 5 to 18.	www.bbbsa.org

References

Kinnaman, David. UnChristian: What a New Generation Really Thinks about Christianity... and Why It Matters. Grand Rapids, MI: Baker Publishing Group, September 30, 2007.

Moore, Beth. Living Beyond Yourself: Exploring the Fruit Of The Spirit. Nashville, TN: Lifeway Publishing, May 2004.

Tacket, Dale. <u>The Truth Project</u>. Colorado Springs, CO: Focus on the Family, 2004.

Ong, Kent. "I Like Your Christ, I Don't Like Your Christians". Honor 2 God. April 10, 2009 <www.honor2god.org>.

Eisley, Lauren. "Starfish Story". Starrbrite. January 4, 2009 <www.starrbrite.com/starfish>.

West, Norris P.. "Volunteering Produces Health Benefits". Americorps. July, 2008 <http://www.americorps.gov/about/newsroom/releases_detail.asp?tbl_pr_id =687 >.

Frazier PHD, Ron. "Volunteer for Better Health". Natural Health and Wellness Magazine. July, 2008 < . http://www.lestout.com/article/health-beauty-fitness/natural-health-wellness/volunteer_better_health.html >.

Angelou, Maya. "Maya Angelou". Red Room. June, 2008 < http://www.redroom.com/author/maya-angelou >.

Gutwein, Austin. "Hoops of Hope". Hoops of Hope. March, 2009 < <u>http://www.hoopsofhope.org/index.cfm</u>>.

Johnson, Jeri. "Young Mothers Serving Others". Young Mothers Serving Others. October, 2009 <http://youngmothersservingothers.blogspot.com/2009/10/donate-laptop-to-one-laptop-per-child.html >.

Johnson - Lewis, Jone. "The Best Way to Find Yourself". Wisdom Quotes. September, 2008 < - http://www.wisdomquotes.com/cat_service.html>.

McNeish, Robert. "Lessons from the Geese". Suewidemark.com. February, 2009 <http://suewidemark.com/lessonsgeese.htm#nutshell>.

McGrann, Patrick. "The Kitegang". The Kitegang. April, 2009 <http://www.kitegang.org/ >.

Embleton, Paul. "BRAVE Foundation". BRAVE Foundation. April, 2009 < http://bravefoundation.org/>.

Sewell Jr., Victor Hugo. "Miracles". Narcotics Anonymous Way of Life. December, 2008 < http://www.nawol.org/2008_ch24%20MIRACLES.htm >.

Author Unknown. "Wikipedia : /Compassion". Wikipedia. January, 2009 < http://en.wikipedia.org/wiki/Compassion >

Author Unknown. "The Greatest Commandment and the Parable of the Good Samaritan". Christian Bible Reference. July, 2008 < http://www.twopaths.com/greatest.htm >.

Schlatter, John. "Kyle's Story". Chicken Soup for the Soul. May, 2008 <http://www.breakthechain.org/exclusives/kyle.html>.

Galozzi, Chuck. "What Makes You Happy - The Attitude of Gratitude - I Am Thankful". Personal Development.com. August, 2008 <http://personal-development.com/chuck/what-makes-you-happy.htm>.

Swindoll, Charles. "Vision". Think Exist. July, 2008 <http://thinkexist.com/quotes/charles_r._swindoll/>.

Keller, Helen. "Character". Think Exist. July, 2008 <http://thinkexist.com/quotation/character-is-like-the-fire-within-the-flint/411292.html >.

Author Unknown. "Feed Each Other". Poetic Expressions. December, 2007
< . http://www.poeticexpressions.co.uk/FeedEachOther.htm>.

The Early Show, "Donation Kept On Giving - Four Lives Saved, Eight
People Linked by One Selfless Act". CBS Interactive Inc. October, 2008
<http://www.cbsnews.com/stories/2008/08/06/earlyshow/main4324353.sht
ml>.

Author Unknown, "He Needed Me". Equilibrium World. February, 2009
<http://equilibrium2008.wordpress.com/2009/09/27/>.

By permission. From *Merriam-Webster's Collegiate® Dictionary, 11th
Edition©2010* by Merriam-Webster, Incorporated (www.Merriam-
Webster.com).

Author Unknown, "A Dog's Purpose - Lessons from a Six Year Old".
Archive Constant Contact. April, 2009
<http://archive.constantcontact.com/fs020/1102009605628/archive/1102431
279183.html>.

Lewis, CS. "You Don't Have a Soul". Brainy Quote. June, 2008
<www.brainyquote.com>.

My Serving Goals / Ideas

Made in the USA
Charleston, SC
10 September 2012